Editor
Marisa Maccarelli-Harris, M.A.

Managing Editor
Mara Ellen Guckian

Editor in Chief
Karen J. Goldfluss, M.S. Ed.

Creative Director
Sarah M. Smith

Cover Artist
Barb Lorseyedi

Art Coordinator
Renée Mc Elwee

Imaging
James Edward Grace
Craig Gunnell

Publisher
Mary D. Smith, M.S. Ed.

Authors

Sandra Cook, M.A.
Helen Leon, M.A.

For correlations to the Common Core State Standards, see pages 8–9.
Correlations can also be found at
http://www.teachercreated.com/standards/

Teacher Created Resources
6421 Industry Way
Westminster, CA 92683
www.teachercreated.com

ISBN: 978-1-4206-3952-0

© *2014 Teacher Created Resources*
Made in U.S.A.

Table of Contents

Introduction

It is Wednesday afternoon and the teacher has just announced a math test for Friday. Across the classroom, hearts start to race. Looks of dread appear on the faces of the students. Taking a test can be very stressful. Can you remember a time when you studied very hard and thought you knew everything, but you received the test results and were shocked to see a grade that was much lower than you had expected? What happened? Well, you might have known the material, but there is more to taking a test than just knowing the material. To be successful when taking a test, you must also know test-taking strategies.

Taking tests is not something new, but the number of tests taken by a student and the importance of those tests is. This math problem-solving book focuses on the skills included in the Common Core State Standards that are prevalent on standardized, multiple-choice tests. This book concentrates on understanding the various types of math problems that may be presented for a particular skill and how to evaluate the problems in order to solve them. From preparing students to recognize tricky questions designed to confuse them, to exercises that emphasize the importance of discriminating necessary facts from unnecessary ones, this book gives students the tools and the experience to enable them to critically analyze and solve grade-level-appropriate math problems.

Students will learn test-taking skills needed to become more confident and efficient test takers. Furthermore, students will gain critical-thinking skills that can be used in many situations throughout their test-taking years and beyond.

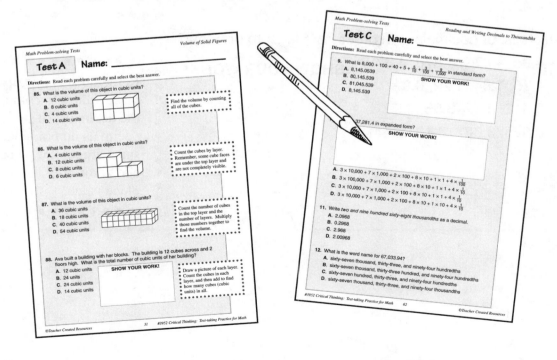

How the Book Is Organized

This book is organized into three tests: Test A, Test B, and Test C. Each test has 100 questions that are aligned to the new Common Core State Standards. Different types of questions are included to familiarize students with strategies that are crucial to successful test taking.

There are four questions on each page of the three tests. For continuity, the skill is the same for each question number across all three tests, which means, for example, that question 14 tests the same skill on Test A as it does on Test B and Test C. These assessments were designed so that the degree of call-out assistance provided decreases from Test A to Test B, with no call outs on Test C.

Test A

Test A provides students with specific and detailed guidance regarding how to approach each math problem. Call-outs appear as rectangular-shaped boxes that are positioned beside the questions. These call-outs give the students specific information to help solve the problem.

Example from Test A

Directions: Read each problem carefully and select the best answer.

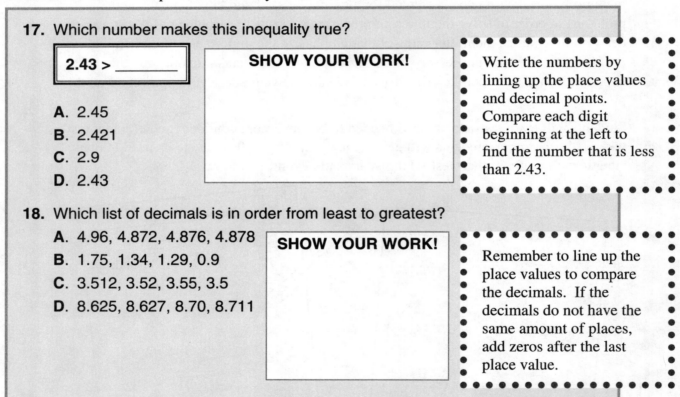

17. Which number makes this inequality true?

2.43 > _____

SHOW YOUR WORK!

A. 2.45
B. 2.421
C. 2.9
D. 2.43

Write the numbers by lining up the place values and decimal points. Compare each digit beginning at the left to find the number that is less than 2.43.

18. Which list of decimals is in order from least to greatest?

A. 4.96, 4.872, 4.876, 4.878
B. 1.75, 1.34, 1.29, 0.9
C. 3.512, 3.52, 3.55, 3.5
D. 8.625, 8.627, 8.70, 8.711

SHOW YOUR WORK!

Remember to line up the place values to compare the decimals. If the decimals do not have the same amount of places, add zeros after the last place value.

How the Book Is Organized (cont.)

Example from Test A (cont.)

Test A offers assistance to properly "decode" each question. Work with students throughout this test and encourage critical thinking. Try these strategies:

- Have students underline important facts in order to draw attention to their importance in the solution of the problem.

- Highlight or circle clue words or phrases to help students focus on choosing the correct operation needed to solve the problem.

- Go over the test as a group, reviewing it line by line in order to help interpret each problem and each possible answer.

Consider the examples from Test A. You might underline ">" and "least to greatest" because the information is critical to finding the problems' solutions.

Test B

Test B continues to provide call-out support, but there are fewer call-outs. Test B is another opportunity for students to practice test-taking strategies, such as underlining important facts and highlighting or circling key words and phrases. It offers the teacher a chance to assess which math skills still need additional work.

Example from Test B

Directions: Read each problem carefully and select the best answer.

17. Which number comes between 8.36 and 8.37?

    A. 8.366

    B. 8.360

    C. 8.371

    D. 8.38

    SHOW YOUR WORK!

    Add zeros so the decimals have the same number of places: 8.36*0*, _____, 8.37*0*.

18. Which list of decimals is in order from greatest to least?

    A. 5.788, 5.878, 5.88, 5.9

    B. 9.822, 0.999, 9.908, 9.999

    C. 0.631, 0.613, 0.603, 0.6

    D. 2.3, 2.31, 2.33, 2.39

How the Book Is Organized *(cont.)*

Test C

Test C also provides 100 questions, but no call-out support is provided. It is an opportunity for students to take a math problem-solving assessment independently. This test will give both you and your students an opportunity to see the degree to which they have internalized not only the ability to correctly identify skills needed to solve the problem, but the specific strategies they can employ to answer each question.

Answer Key

The answer key at the back of this book is designed to be another test-taking tool for both teachers and students. A student bubble sheet is also provided on page 112.

While it is important for students to know which answer is correct, it is equally useful for students to understand why other options are incorrect. The answer key provides explanations for the correct answers to the questions. Each incorrect answer is also discussed to provide students with possible explanations for why they might have chosen it.

The following example from the answer key shows the answer to question 17 from Test B on the previous page.

Sample Answer Key Explanation

17. Correct Answer: C

Ignore the decimal points to compare: 0.<u>631</u> > 0.<u>613</u> > 0.<u>603</u> > 0.6<u>00</u>.

Incorrect Answers:

A. The correct order is 5.9, 5.88, 5.878, 5.788.

B. The correct order is 9.999, 9.908, 9.822, 0.999.

D. 2.3, 2.31, 2.33, 2.39 are in order from least to greatest, not greatest to least.

How to Use the Book

Teachers know that students learn differently. Each class tends to be strong in some skill areas and weak in others. Therefore, it is up to the teacher to decide how to use this book to best benefit the students. Consider the following possibilities:

The book can be completed in the order it has been written. Test A can be completed first, then Test B, and finally Test C. Teachers will lend less support in Test B than in Test A, and Test C can be administered as a true test to assess students' skills.

The book can also be completed in smaller increments, depending on the needs of the class. Since each test has 100 questions, consider dividing the tests into parts. For example, assign problems 1–20 on Test A. Carefully review the questions on this test, along with the call-outs, with the class. Assign the same 20 questions on Test B and review the responses as a group. Finally, assign questions 1–20 on Test C. Test C does not contain any call-outs; students should complete it independently. After completing Test C independently, each question can be reviewed orally and modeled, if necessary, so the students can understand why each answer is correct or incorrect. Any observed weaknesses should be addressed as they arise. Another approach to Test C would be for the teacher to collect and grade the test after students independently complete it. Any areas of weakness should be reviewed and modeled as a class or in a small-group setting.

All answers should be reviewed so students know why an answer was incorrect. Make this an appealing activity by creating a classroom full of detectives. When reviewing answers to the questions, have each student come up with a reason why someone would make that error. For example, the student might state that the problem was wrong because the number facts were added instead of subtracted. Finding the reason for the incorrect answer will help students understand the problem and solve the mystery.

In addition, the tests can be used as study tools. Place the tests and answer sheets in a binder that is accessible to students. They can "self-test" before and between assessments (including standardized tests) to maintain skills and focus on test-taking strategies.

Common Core State Standards Correlation

Each question in *Critical Thinking: Test-taking Practice for Math (Grade 5)* meets one or more of the following Common Core State Standards© Copyright 2010. National Governors Association Center for Best Practices and Council of Chief State School Officers. All rights reserved. For more information about these standards, go to *http://www.corestandards.org/* or *http://www.teachercreated.com/standards/*.

Operations & Algebraic Thinking	Problem #s
Math.5.OA.A.1 Use parentheses, brackets, or braces in numerical expressions, and evaluate expressions with these symbols.	37–44
Number & Operations in Base Ten	
Math.5.NBT.A.1 Recognize that in a multi-digit number, a digit in one place represents 10 times as much as it represents in the place to its right and $\frac{1}{10}$ of what it represents in the place to its left.	15–16
Math.5.NBT.A.3 Read, write, and compare decimals to thousandths.	13–14
Math.5.NBT.A.3a Read and write decimals to thousandths using base-ten numerals, number names, and expanded form.	9–12
Math.5.NBT.A.3b Compare two decimals to thousandths based on meanings of the digits in each place, using >, =, and < symbols to record results of comparison.	17–20
Math.5.NBT.A.4 Use place value understanding to round decimals to any place.	21–24
Math.5.NBT.B.5 Fluently multiply multi-digit whole numbers using the standard algorithm.	1–4
Math.5.NBT.B.6 Find whole-number quotients of whole numbers with up to four-digit dividends and two-digit divisors, using strategies based on place value, the properties of operations, and/or the relationship between multiplication and division. Illustrate and explain the calculation by using equations, rectangular arrays, and/or area models.	5–8
Math.5.NBT.B.7 Add, subtract, multiply, and divide decimals to hundredths, using concrete models or drawings and strategies based on place value, properties of operations, and/or the relationship between addition and subtraction; relate the strategy to a written method and explain reasoning used.	25–28, 29–32 33–36
Number & Operations — Fractions	
Math.5.NF.A.1 Add and subtract fractions with unlike denominators (including mixed numbers) by replacing given fractions with equivalent fractions in such a way as to produce an equivalent sum or difference of fractions with like denominators.	45–48, 49–52, 53–56
Math.5.NF.A.2 Solve word problems involving addition and subtraction of fractions referring to the same whole, including cases of unlike denominators, e.g., by using visual fraction models or equations to represent the problem.	49–52, 53–56

Test A | Name: _____

Directions: Read each problem carefully and select the best answer.

21. What is 7,603.6819 rounded to the nearest thousand?
    A. 7,603.68
    B. 8,000
    C. 7,000
    D. 7,603.682

    > Underline the digit that is in the thousands place. Look at the digit to the right of it. If the digit is 5 or greater, round up. If the digit is 4 or less, round down.

22. What is 44.209 rounded to the nearest tenth?
    A. 44.3
    B. 44.2
    C. 44.21
    D. 40.0

    > The number directly to the right of the decimal is the tenths place.

23. When rounded to the nearest tenth, Marco has about $15.50 in his pocket. Which of the amounts below could be the actual amount of money that Marco has in his pocket?
    A. $15.44
    B. $15.54
    C. $15.55
    D. $15.50

    > $15.50 is already rounded to the nearest tenth. Which amount, when rounded to the nearest tenth, is $15.50?

24. Kate bought a purse for $15.56. What is the price of the purse to the nearest dollar?
    A. $15.60
    B. $20.00
    C. $15.00
    D. $16.00

    > Round to the *nearest dollar* by rounding the number in the *ones* place.

Test A | Name: _____

Directions: Read each problem carefully and select the best answer.

25. Which value makes the addition sentence true?

| 14.4 + 3.58 = ___ |

SHOW YOUR WORK!

A. 5.02

B. 50.2

C. 1.789

D. 17.98

> Line up the decimal points.
> Add a zero to 14.4 so that
> both numbers have the same
> amount of digits after the
> decimal point.

26. Which value makes the subtraction sentence true?

| 8.5 – 6.27 = ___ |

SHOW YOUR WORK!

A. 2.37

B. 2.23

C. 6.58

D. 65.8

> Don't forget to line up the
> decimals. Add a zero after
> 8.5 so that both numbers
> have the same amount of
> digits after the decimal point.

27. Karen weighs 82.35 lb. Dina weighs 85.25 lb. How many more pounds does Dina weigh than Karen?

A. 2.90 lb.

B. 167.60 lb.

C. 3.90 lb.

D. 0.290 lb.

SHOW YOUR WORK!

> *How many more* is a clue to
> help you choose which
> operation to use.

28. Jeff ran 2.5 km. Justin ran 3.81 km. How many kilometers did Jeff and Justin run all together?

A. 1.31 km

B. 63.1 km

C. 6.31 km

D. 4.06 km

SHOW YOUR WORK!

> *All together* is a clue that
> means to combine. What
> operation is used to combine
> amounts?

Test A   Name: _____

Directions: Read each problem carefully and select the best answer.

29. Which value makes the multiplication sentence true?

| 5.2 × 3.7 = ___ |

SHOW YOUR WORK!

A. 192.4
B. 8.9
C. 19.24
D. 1.924

Count the *total* number of places to the right of the decimal in both factors. Starting at the right of the product, count that many places to the left and put the decimal point there.

30. Which value makes the division sentence true?

| 6.25 ÷ 0.5 = ___ |

SHOW YOUR WORK!

A. 12.5
B. 1.25
C. 0.125
D. 0.08

Move the decimal one place to the right in the divisor. Now move the decimal point one place to the right in the dividend. That is where the decimal will be in the quotient.

31. Bob jumped rope for 9.36 minutes. Each jump took 0.2 minutes. How many times did Bob jump?

A. 1.872 times
B. 0.468 times
C. 4.68 times
D. 46.8 times

SHOW YOUR WORK!

Which operation can be used to split the total amount of time into groups of equal size (0.2 minutes each)?

32. Jessica paid $0.48 for each bag of beads. She bought 6 bags. How much did Jessica pay all together for the beads?

A. $0.08
B. $2.88
C. $0.54
D. $0.42

SHOW YOUR WORK!

All together is a clue for addition or multiplication. Which operation will solve this problem more quickly?

Test A

Name: _____

Directions: Read the word problem carefully. Select the best answer for each question.

Carol has 5.36 pints of strawberries, 4.82 pints of blueberries, and 3.49 pints of raspberries. She uses 3.25 pints of the berries to make a fruit salad. How many pints of berries does Carol have left?

33. What do you need to calculate first to solve the problem?

    A. how many pints of strawberries Carol will use

    B. how many pints of each type of berry Carol will use

    C. how many pints of berries Carol has in all

    D. what Carol will do with the rest of the berries

> Think about it. You cannot find what you have left if you do not know the total amount you started with.

34. What is the answer for step one?

    A. 16.92 pints of berries

    B. 10.18 pints of berries

    C. 13.43 pints of berries

    D. 13.67 pints of berries

SHOW YOUR WORK!

> You need to find how many pints of berries Carol has *all together*.

35. What clue helps you decide what operation is needed to solve step two of the problem?

    A. how many pints of berries

    B. have left

    C. does Carol have

    D. make a fruit salad

> Which clue tells you to find the *difference*?

36. What is the answer to the word problem?

    A. 10.42 pints of berries

    B. 16.92 pints of berries

    C. 104.2 pints of berries

    D. 10.42 pints of fruit salad

SHOW YOUR WORK!

> Does your answer make sense? Is the decimal point in the right place?

Test A   Name: _____

Directions: Read each problem carefully and select the best answer.

37. Which value makes the number sentence true?

| $(6 \times 5) + (10 - 3) =$ ___ |

SHOW YOUR WORK!

A. 210
B. 18
C. 37
D. 30

> Do the computations inside the parentheses first.

38. Which value makes the number sentence true?

| $2^3 \times (9 + 7) =$ ___ |

SHOW YOUR WORK!

A. 128
B. 96
C. 64
D. 79

> Parentheses first, then exponents.

39. Simplify.

| $(24 \div 6) \times 3 + 5$ |

SHOW YOUR WORK!

A. 27
B. 32
C. 12
D. 17

> Simplify what is in parentheses first. Then, follow the *order of operations* to simplify everything else: exponents, multiplication and division (left to right), and addition and subtraction (left to right).

40. Which number sentence is true when $n = 4$?

A. $(n + 3) \times (5 - 3) = 9$
B. $(7 + 2) \div (3 \times 1) + n = 7$
C. $(6 \times 3) + n + 3^2 = 28$
D. $n + (63 \div 9) \times 5 = 55$

SHOW YOUR WORK!

> Replace *n* with 4, and remember to simplify what is inside of parentheses first. Then follow the *order of operations*.

Test A   Name: _____

Directions: Read each problem carefully and select the best answer.

41. Which value makes the number sentence true?

$$4 \times [(3 + 5) \times (12 - 7)] = \underline{\hspace{1cm}}$$

A. 40

B. 160

C. 356

D. 32

SHOW YOUR WORK!

Do the computations inside the parentheses first, then simplify what's left inside the brackets.

42. Simplify.

$$[(8^2 \div 4) + (3 \times 9)] - 6$$

A. 25

B. 43

C. 23

D. 37

SHOW YOUR WORK!

First find the value of the number with the exponent.

43. Simplify.

$$[7 \times (45 \div 9)] + 236$$

A. 1,687

B. 8,260

C. 271

D. 35

SHOW YOUR WORK!

Operations inside parentheses are always done first. Then, simplify what's left inside the brackets.

44. Evaluate the expression for $n = 2$.

$$n \times [(2.3 \times 7.1) - (4.21 + 9.8)]$$

A. 2.32

B. 38.25

C. 18.65

D. 4.64

SHOW YOUR WORK!

Follow these steps to solve:

1. parentheses

2. brackets

3. multiply

Test A   Name: _____

Directions: Read each problem carefully and select the best answer.

45. Rename the fractions $\frac{2}{5}$ and $\frac{3}{4}$ to equivalent fractions with a common denominator.

   A. $\frac{4}{20}$ and $\frac{5}{20}$

   B. $\frac{2}{20}$ and $\frac{3}{20}$

   C. $\frac{2}{5}$ and $\frac{3}{5}$

   D. $\frac{8}{20}$ and $\frac{15}{20}$

> **SHOW YOUR WORK!**

> Remember to list the multiples of both of the denominators to find the least common multiple to use as the fractions' common denominator.

46. Julia wants to add $\frac{3}{5}$ and $\frac{2}{3}$, so first she must find equivalent fractions with a common denominator. Which pair of fractions could Julia use to add $\frac{3}{5}$ and $\frac{2}{3}$?

   A. $\frac{9}{15}$ and $\frac{2}{15}$

   B. $\frac{3}{15}$ and $\frac{5}{15}$

   C. $\frac{9}{15}$ and $\frac{10}{15}$

   D. $\frac{3}{5}$ and $\frac{2}{5}$

> **SHOW YOUR WORK!**

> Be careful! Be sure to rename both the numerator and denominator.

47. Find a common denominator for the fractions $\frac{3}{4}$ and $\frac{2}{3}$.

   A. 7

   B. 8

   C. 12

   D. 6

> **SHOW YOUR WORK!**

> Think about it! Use a common multiple as the denominator.

48. Nick completes the first lap of the BMX bicycle race in $\frac{5}{6}$ of a minute and the second lap in $\frac{3}{4}$ of a minute. In order to find his average speed for laps one and two, Nick must first add his times together. Which pair of fractions could Nick use to find his average time?

   A. $\frac{5}{12}$ and $\frac{3}{12}$

   B. $\frac{10}{12}$ and $\frac{9}{12}$

   C. $\frac{2}{12}$ and $\frac{3}{12}$

   D. $\frac{10}{12}$ and $\frac{3}{12}$

> **SHOW YOUR WORK!**

> Remember to multiply the numerator and denominator of each fraction by the same number.

Test A   Name: _____

Directions: Read each problem carefully and select the best answer. Answers should be in simplest form.

---

49. Nicole lives on a ranch and is in charge of feeding the smaller animals every morning. She prepares the feed by combining $\frac{1}{5}$ cup of flax seeds and $\frac{3}{6}$ cup of oats for each animal. How much feed does each animal receive?

A. $\frac{9}{30}$ of a cup

B. $\frac{7}{10}$ of a cup

C. $\frac{21}{30}$ of a cup

D. $\frac{22}{30}$ of a cup

SHOW YOUR WORK!

Remember to find a common denominator before solving the problem.

50. Samantha is a great artist. She often mixes different colored paints to create certain shades or colors. She mixed $\frac{2}{3}$ cups of yellow paint and $\frac{1}{4}$ cup of blue paint to make green paint. How much paint does she have?

A. $\frac{11}{12}$ cup

B. $\frac{12}{12}$ cup

C. $\frac{5}{12}$ cup

D. $\frac{3}{4}$ cup

SHOW YOUR WORK!

Be careful! The numerator and the denominator of each fraction must be multiplied by the same number to find an equivalent fraction.

51. Andrew needs to fill the lawn mower with a gas and oil mixture. He will mix $\frac{4}{8}$ of a quart of gas with $\frac{3}{12}$ of a quart of oil. How much more gas than oil will he use?

A. $\frac{12}{24}$ of a quart

B. $\frac{3}{4}$ of a quart

C. $\frac{7}{20}$ of a quart

D. $\frac{1}{4}$ of a quart

SHOW YOUR WORK!

Read the problem carefully to determine the correct operation to use.

52. Julia made $\frac{3}{4}$ gallon of punch. She drank $\frac{3}{12}$ gallon of punch. How much punch does she have left to share?

A. $\frac{6}{12}$ gallon

B. 1 gallon

C. $\frac{1}{2}$ gallon

D. $\frac{7}{12}$ gallon

SHOW YOUR WORK!

Find a common denominator, subtract the numerators, and write the difference on top of the common denominator.

Test A   Name: _____

Directions: Read each problem carefully and select the best answer. Answers should be in simplest form.

53. Luca is gathering materials for his science project. Step one of the directions requires a piece of string $8\frac{4}{12}$ inches long, and step two of the directions requires a piece of string $3\frac{1}{3}$ inches long. How many inches of string does Luca need in all for his science project?

A. $11\frac{5}{15}$ inches

B. 5 inches

C. $11\frac{8}{12}$ inches

D. $11\frac{2}{3}$ inches

SHOW YOUR WORK!

Remember to add the numerators, and write the sum over a common denominator.

54. The cheerleading squad made $4\frac{5}{8}$ gallons of lemonade to sell at the basketball game. They sold $2\frac{7}{8}$ gallons. How many gallons were not sold?

A. $2\frac{1}{4}$ gallons

B. $1\frac{6}{8}$ gallons

C. $1\frac{3}{4}$ gallons

D. $7\frac{1}{2}$ gallons

SHOW YOUR WORK!

Rename a fraction to solve.

55. Danny has $5\frac{5}{6}$ bags of sand. If he uses $4\frac{1}{2}$ bags of the sand for his sandbox, how much sand will he have left over?

A. $1\frac{2}{6}$ bags

B. $1\frac{1}{3}$ bags

C. $9\frac{8}{6}$ bags

D. $1\frac{2}{3}$ bags

SHOW YOUR WORK!

Look back! Did you use the correct operation to solve the problem?

56. Nicholas surfed for $2\frac{3}{4}$ hours on Saturday and $2\frac{3}{8}$ hours on Sunday. How many hours did Nicholas surf in all?

A. $4\frac{9}{8}$ hours

B. $\frac{3}{8}$ hour

C. $5\frac{1}{8}$ hours

D. $4\frac{6}{12}$ hours

SHOW YOUR WORK!

In all is a clue that tells what operation to use to solve.

Test A   Name: _____

Directions: Read each problem carefully and select the best answer. Answers should be in simplest form.

57. Find the product.

$\dfrac{2}{5} \times \dfrac{5}{8}$

A. $\dfrac{10}{40}$

B. $\dfrac{7}{13}$

C. $\dfrac{7}{40}$

D. $\dfrac{1}{4}$

SHOW YOUR WORK!

Remember to multiply numerators together and denominators together.

58. Multiply.

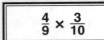

$\dfrac{4}{9} \times \dfrac{3}{10}$

A. $\dfrac{12}{90}$

B. $\dfrac{2}{15}$

C. $\dfrac{4}{30}$

D. $\dfrac{7}{19}$

SHOW YOUR WORK!

Remember to reduce.

59. The Parent Teacher Association is sponsoring a fundraiser for the school. $\dfrac{3}{4}$ of the money raised will be used to improve the playground. $\dfrac{2}{3}$ of the playground money will be used to buy new playground equipment. What fraction of the total money raised will be used to purchase new playground equipment?

A. $\dfrac{6}{12}$ of the money

B. $\dfrac{5}{7}$ of the money

C. $\dfrac{1}{2}$ of the money

D. $\dfrac{5}{12}$ of the money

SHOW YOUR WORK!

Understand the problem before solving. Did you use the correct operation? Hint: *Of* suggests multiplication.

60. Chrissie and Angie ordered a large pizza. Chrissie ate $\dfrac{1}{2}$ as much pizza as Angie. If Angie ate $\dfrac{2}{8}$ of the pizza, how much pizza did Chrissie eat?

A. $\dfrac{2}{16}$ of the pizza

B. $\dfrac{3}{10}$ of the pizza

C. $\dfrac{1}{8}$ of the pizza

D. $\dfrac{3}{4}$ of the pizza

SHOW YOUR WORK!

Remember, when *multiplying* fractions there is *no addition*.

Test A   Name: _____

Directions: Read each problem carefully and select the best answer. Answers should be in simplest form.

61. Find $\frac{3}{4}$ of 25.

A. $18\frac{3}{4}$

B. $\frac{75}{4}$

C. $\frac{28}{5}$

D. $\frac{3}{100}$

SHOW YOUR WORK!

Remember *of* means to *multiply* in math word problems.

62. Sandy and Helen were selling chocolate candy bars. Sandy sold 3 times as many bars as Helen. If Helen sold $\frac{1}{2}$ a box of candy bars, how many boxes of candy bars did Sandy sell?

A. $\frac{1}{6}$ box

B. $\frac{3}{2}$ boxes

C. $3\frac{1}{2}$ boxes

D. $1\frac{1}{2}$ boxes

SHOW YOUR WORK!

Remember to write your answer as a mixed number.

63. Find the product.

$$35 \times \frac{2}{7}$$

A. $\frac{70}{7}$

B. $\frac{2}{245}$

C. 10

D. $\frac{245}{2}$

SHOW YOUR WORK!

Think about it. Multiply the whole number by the numerator.

64. Richard has 9 acres of land. He grows grapes on $\frac{3}{4}$ of his land. How many acres of land does he grow grapes on?

A. $9\frac{3}{4}$ acres

B. $\frac{1}{12}$ acre

C. $\frac{27}{4}$ acres

D. $6\frac{3}{4}$ acres

SHOW YOUR WORK!

Take a quick look. Did you make the whole number an improper fraction?

Test A   Name: _____

Directions: Read each problem carefully and select the best answer. Answers should be in simplest form.

65. Divide.

$$9 \div \frac{3}{7}$$

A. $3\frac{6}{7}$

B. $\frac{1}{21}$

C. 21

D. $\frac{3}{7}$

SHOW YOUR WORK!

Remember to use the reciprocal of the number *after* the division sign.

66. The snack bar on the beach often mixes lemonade with iced tea to make a refreshing drink. Today, a $\frac{1}{2}$ gallon of lemonade will be mixed with 4 gallons of iced tea. How much lemonade will be mixed with each of gallon of iced tea?

A. 8 gallons

B. 2 gallons

C. $\frac{1}{2}$ gallon

D. $\frac{1}{8}$ gallon

SHOW YOUR WORK!

Take a look at the question. Did you put the numbers in the correct order to solve?

67. Find the quotient.

$$\frac{5}{8} \div 5$$

A. $\frac{1}{9}$

B. $\frac{1}{8}$

C. $3\frac{1}{8}$

D. $\frac{5}{40}$

SHOW YOUR WORK!

Pay attention! Division problems with fractions are turned into multiplication problems.

68. In the summertime, Kris often makes corn on the cob on the outside grill. He seasons the corn with butter and salt. If he seasons 6 pieces of corn evenly with $\frac{3}{4}$ ounce of salt, how much salt will he put on each piece of corn?

A. 8 ounces

B. $4\frac{1}{2}$ ounces

C. $\frac{1}{2}$ ounce

D. $\frac{1}{8}$ ounce

SHOW YOUR WORK!

Think about which number is being divided up into parts; that will be the first number in the division problem.

| Test A | Name: _____ |

Directions: Read each problem carefully and select the best answer. Answers should be in simplest form.

69. The butcher wants to cut a $\frac{3}{4}$ pound roast into three equal steaks. How much will each steak weigh?

- **A.** $\frac{3}{12}$ pound
- **B.** $\frac{1}{4}$ pound
- **C.** 4 pounds
- **D.** $2\frac{1}{4}$ pounds

SHOW YOUR WORK!

The roast is being cut into three equal-sized steaks. What operation should be used to *cut up* the whole?

70. Wanda had $\frac{1}{2}$ a bottle of orange juice. She wanted to serve an equal amount of juice to each of her four nieces with breakfast. How much juice will each of Wanda's nieces have with breakfast?

- **A.** 2 bottles of juice
- **B.** 8 bottles of juice
- **C.** $\frac{1}{8}$ bottle of juice
- **D.** $\frac{1}{2}$ bottle of juice

SHOW YOUR WORK!

Don't forget to multiply by the reciprocal when dividing with fractions.

71. Steve collected $\frac{4}{5}$ barrel of aluminum cans to be recycled. Todd collected 5 times as much. How many barrels of aluminum cans did Todd collect?

- **A.** $\frac{4}{25}$ barrel
- **B.** 4 barrels
- **C.** $\frac{20}{5}$ barrels
- **D.** 5 barrels

SHOW YOUR WORK!

Remember, to turn a whole number into an improper fraction, write it over 1.

72. Grandpa Leon took his five grandchildren to the lake for a picnic. They were at the lake for 5 hours. They spent $\frac{1}{4}$ of their time on rented paddleboats. How much time did they spend on the paddleboats that day?

- **A.** $5\frac{1}{4}$ hours
- **B.** $\frac{1}{20}$ hour
- **C.** $\frac{5}{4}$ hours
- **D.** $1\frac{1}{4}$ hours

SHOW YOUR WORK!

Use what you know! The word *of* in a math word problem means to *multiply*.

Test A   Name: _____

Directions: Read each problem carefully and select the best answer.

73. Which measurement is equal to 9 yd.?

A. 108 in.

B. 24 ft.

C. 324 in.

D. 27 ft. and 9 in.

SHOW YOUR WORK!

36 inches = 1 yard. *Multiply* when converting from larger to smaller units.

74. Which measurement is equal to 5,000 g?

A. 50 kg

B. 5,000,000 mg

C. 50,000 mg

D. 500 kg

SHOW YOUR WORK!

1 gram = 1,000 milligrams and 1,000 grams = 1 kilogram. Remember to *multiply* to convert from larger to smaller units and *divide* to convert from smaller to larger units.

75. Brandon is supplying the juice for his soccer team. There are 12 players on his team. Each player will drink 500 mL of juice. How many liters of juice should Brandon bring for his soccer team?

A. $41\frac{2}{3}$ mL

B. 5 L

C. 5 L and 500 mL

D. 6 L

SHOW YOUR WORK!

1,000 milliliters = 1 liter. *Divide* to convert from smaller to larger units.

76. A table weighs $64\frac{1}{2}$ pounds. How many ounces is that?

A. 1,032 oz.

B. 1,024 oz.

C. 774 oz.

D. about 4 oz.

SHOW YOUR WORK!

1 pound = 16 ounces

$\frac{1}{2}$ pound = 8 ounces

Test A   Name: _____

Directions: Read each problem carefully and select the best answer.

Use the grid to answer questions 77 and 78.

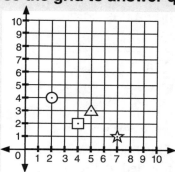

77. Which shape is located at (2,4) on the grid?

    A. triangle   **B.** square   **C.** circle   **D.** star

> Start at 0. Move 2 spaces to the right. Then move 4 spaces up. What shape do you see?

78. Which shape is located at (5,3) on the grid?

    A. triangle   **B.** square   **C.** circle   **D.** star

Use the grid to answer questions 79 and 80.

> The first number tells how far to move to the right. The second number tells how far to move up.

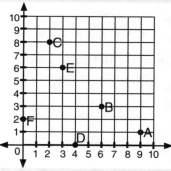

79. What is the ordered pair for point *B*?

    A. (3,6)   **B.** (2,8)   **C.** (0,2)   **D.** (6,3)

> Count to the *right* until you are under the B. Then count *up* to the B.

80. What is the ordered pair for point *D*?

    A. (2,8)   **B.** (4,0)   **C.** (0,2)   **D.** (9,1)

> Remember, the first coordinate tells how far right from 0 the point is, and the second coordinate tells how far up from 0 the point is.

Test A	Name: _____

Directions: Read each problem carefully and select the best answer.

Use the information below to answer questions 81–84.

The Boy Scouts sold candy to raise money for a camping trip. The values below show how many pounds of candy each Scout sold.

$4\frac{1}{2}, 6\frac{1}{2},\ 7,\ 5\frac{1}{2}, 4\frac{1}{2}, 8\frac{1}{2}, 4\frac{1}{2}, 6\frac{1}{2}, 7\frac{1}{2},\ 5,\ \ 7,\ 6\frac{1}{2}, 5\frac{1}{2}, 3\frac{1}{2}, 7\frac{1}{2}, 6\frac{1}{2}, 8\frac{1}{2}, 5\frac{1}{2}, 4\frac{1}{2}, 7\frac{1}{2}$

81. What are the greatest and least numbers of pounds of candy?

    A. greatest = $7\frac{1}{2}$ pounds; least = $5\frac{1}{2}$ pounds

    B. greatest = $7\frac{1}{2}$ pounds; least = $4\frac{1}{2}$ pounds

    C. greatest = $8\frac{1}{2}$ pounds; least = 5 pounds

    D. greatest = $8\frac{1}{2}$ pounds; least = $3\frac{1}{2}$ pounds

> This line plot was not finished; the data was not ordered from least to greatest. Look carefully!

SHOW YOUR WORK!

82. How many more Boy Scouts sold $6\frac{1}{2}$ pounds of candy than sold $8\frac{1}{2}$ pounds?

    A. 1 Boy Scout

    B. 2 Boy Scouts

    C. 3 Boy Scouts

    D. 6 Boy Scouts

SHOW YOUR WORK!

> How many times does $6\frac{1}{2}$ appear? What about $8\frac{1}{2}$?

83. How many Boy Scouts sold candy?

    A. 18 Boy Scouts   **C.** 20 Boy Scouts

    B. 21 Boy Scouts   **D.** 19 Boy Scouts

> Count the total number of values given.

84. On a line plot, how many Xs would be above $4\frac{1}{2}$?

    A. 4   **B.** 3   **C.** 5   **D.** 6

> How many times does $4\frac{1}{2}$ appear?

Test A   Name: _____

Directions: Read each problem carefully and select the best answer.

85. What is the volume of this object in cubic units?
  - **A**. 12 cubic units
  - **B**. 8 cubic units
  - **C**. 4 cubic units
  - **D**. 14 cubic units

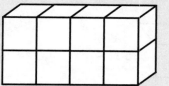

> Find the volume by counting all of the cubes.

86. What is the volume of this object in cubic units?
  - **A**. 4 cubic units
  - **B**. 12 cubic units
  - **C**. 8 cubic units
  - **D**. 6 cubic units

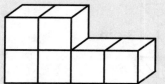

> Count the cubes by layer. Remember, some cube faces are under the top layer and are not completely visible.

87. What is the volume of this object in cubic units?
  - **A**. 36 cubic units
  - **B**. 18 cubic units
  - **C**. 40 cubic units
  - **D**. 54 cubic units

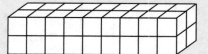

> Count the number of cubes in the top layer and the number of layers. Multiply those numbers together to find the volume.

88. Ava built a building with her blocks. The building is 12 cubes across and 2 floors high. What is the total number of cubic units of her building?
  - **A**. 12 cubic units
  - **B**. 24 units
  - **C**. 24 cubic units
  - **D**. 14 cubic units

SHOW YOUR WORK!

> Draw a picture of each layer. Count the cubes in each layer, and then add to find how many cubes (cubic units) in all.

Test A   Name: _____

Directions: Read each problem carefully and select the best answer.

89. What is the volume of the rectangular prism?

A. 60 ft.^{2}
B. 12 ft.^{3}
C. 60 ft.^{3}
D. 13 ft.^{3}

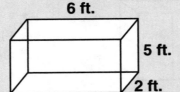

Volume =
length × width × height

90. What is the volume of the rectangular prism?

A. 14 cm^3
B. 84 cm^3
C. 28 cm^3
D. 12 cm^3

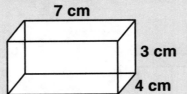

You know the length, width, and height. Use the volume formula to solve.

91. What is the volume of this figure?

A. 84 m^3
B. 504 m^3
C. 98 m^3
D. 90 m^3

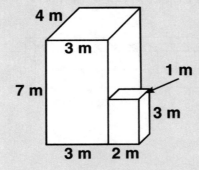

Divide the figure into two rectangular prisms. Find the volume of each one and add them together.

92. What is the volume of this figure?

A. 96 in.^{2}
B. 72 in.^{3}
C. 96 in.^{3}
D. 24 in.^{3}

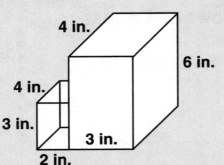

Use $V = l \times w \times h$ to find the volume of each prism. Add the volumes together.

Test B   Name: _____

Directions: Read each problem carefully and select the best answer.

9. What is $70,000 + 1,000 + 600 + 50 + 4 + \frac{2}{10} + \frac{3}{100}$ in standard form?

   A. 71,654.023

   B. 71,654.23

   C. 7,165.423

   D. 71,654.32

   SHOW YOUR WORK!

   > If the value is a fraction, it goes on the right side of the decimal point.

10. What is 4,953.617 in expanded form?

    SHOW YOUR WORK!

    A. $4 \times 1,000 + 9 \times 100 + 5 \times 10 + 3 \times 1 + 6 \times \frac{1}{10} + 1 \times \frac{1}{100} + 7 \times \frac{1}{1,000}$

    B. $4 \times 10,000 + 9 \times 100 + 5 \times 10 + 3 \times 1 + 6 \times \frac{1}{10} + 1 \times \frac{1}{100} + 7 \times \frac{1}{1,000}$

    C. $4 \times 1,000 + 9 \times 100 + 5 \times 10 + 6 \times \frac{1}{1} + 1 \times \frac{1}{10} + 7 \times \frac{1}{100}$

    D. $4 \times 1,000 + 9 \times 100 + 53 \times 10 + 6 \times \frac{1}{10} + 1 \times \frac{1}{100} + 7 \times \frac{1}{1,000}$

11. What is the decimal for *five and thirty-six thousandths*?

    A. 5.36

    B. 0.536

    C. 5.036

    D. 5.0036

    > The word *and* separates the whole number from the decimal.

12. What is the word name for 5,375.281?

    A. five thousand three hundred seventy-five and two hundred eighty-one hundredths

    B. fifty-three thousand seventy-five and two hundred eighty-one thousandths

    C. five thousand three hundred seventy-five and two hundred eighty-one thousandths

    D. five thousand three hundred seventy-five and two hundred eighty-one

Test B	Name: _____

Directions: Read each problem carefully and select the best answer.

13. Which decimal is equal to $1\frac{83}{1,000}$?

A. 1.83

B. 0.183

C. 1.083

D. 1.0083

> **SHOW YOUR WORK!**

14. Which fraction is equal to 7.75? Simplify if possible.

A. $\frac{7}{75}$

B. $7\frac{3}{4}$

C. $\frac{775}{1,000}$

D. $7\frac{1}{4}$

> **SHOW YOUR WORK!**

> Read the decimal out loud, and write the fraction as you say it: *seven and seventy-five hundredths.*

15. How many times less is the value of the digit 7 in 535,870 than the value of the digit 7 in 537,805?

A. 10 times less

B. 100 times less

C. 1,000 times less

D. 2 times less

> **SHOW YOUR WORK!**

> Remember, each place value you move to the left is 10 times greater than the place value to the right.

16. In which decimal is the value of the digit 8 ten times less than the value of the digit 8 in 0.008?

A. 0.08

B. 0.008

C. 0.0008

D. 0.8

> **SHOW YOUR WORK!**

Test B	Name: _____

Directions: Read each problem carefully and select the best answer.

17. Which number comes between 8.36 and 8.37?

A. 8.366
B. 8.360
C. 8.371
D. 8.38

SHOW YOUR WORK!

> Add zeros so the decimals have the same number of places: 8.36*0*, _____, 8.37*0*.

18. Which list of decimals is in order from greatest to least?

A. 5.788, 5.878, 5.88, 5.9
B. 9.822, 0.999, 9.908, 9.999
C. 0.631, 0.613, 0.603, 0.6
D. 2.3, 2.31, 2.33, 2.39

19. Which number makes this inequality true?

1.101 < _____

A. 1.011
B. 1.101
C. 1.01
D. 1.11

SHOW YOUR WORK!

> Put each answer choice in the blank. Compare digit by digit (starting on the left) to find the correct choice.

20. Which number sentence is true?

A. 3.53 > 3.54
B. 6.6 = 6.600
C. 5.8 < 5.76
D. 9.05 = 9.50

Test B   Name: _____

Directions: Read each problem carefully and select the best answer.

21. What is 7.785 rounded to the nearest hundredth?

  A. 7.79

  B. 7.78

  C. 7.8

  D. 8.0

> Underline the digit in the hundredths place, then look at the digit to the right of it. Do you round up or down?

22. Mia weeded her neighbor's garden. She was paid $11.25. How much did Mia earn to the nearest ten cents?

  A. $11.20

  B. $11.00

  C. $10.00

  D. $11.30

23. What is 312.5344 rounded to the nearest thousandth?

  A. 313.0

  B. 312.534

  C. 312.53

  D. 312.5

24. Which number rounds to 68.78 when rounded to the nearest hundredth?

  A. 68.789

  B. 68.779

  C. 68.773

  D. 68.787

> Round each number to the nearest hundredth. Which one rounds to 68.78?

Test B　　Name: _____

Directions: Read each problem carefully and select the best answer.

25. Which value makes the subtraction sentence true?

9.6 – 5.73 = ___

SHOW YOUR WORK!

A. 3.87

B. 38.7

C. 5.23

D. 4.97

> Think about the rules for adding and subtracting decimals. Be sure to line up the numbers correctly.

26. Which value makes the addition sentence true?

52.1 + 65.37 = ___

SHOW YOUR WORK!

A. 70.58

B. 1,174.7

C. 117.47

D. 1.1747

27. The team had 32.5 L of water in their jug to drink during the game. The players drank 27.34 L of water. How many liters of water were left over?

A. 51.6 L

B. 5.16 L

C. 59.84 L

D. 5.24 L

SHOW YOUR WORK!

> *Left over* is a clue phrase to help you identify which operation to use.

28. Dan put 43.99 in. of water in the pool on Tuesday and 42.7 in. of water in the pool on Wednesday. How many inches of water did Dan put in the pool in all?

A. 48.26 in.

B. 1.29 in.

C. 866.9 in.

D. 86.69 in.

SHOW YOUR WORK!

Test B   Name: _____

Directions: Read each problem carefully and select the best answer.

29. Which value makes the division sentence true?

$$16.84 \div 0.4 = \underline{\quad}$$

A. 42.1
B. 4.21
C. 0.421
D. 17.1

SHOW YOUR WORK!

Remember to set up the long division problem correctly; the first number goes *inside* for long division.

30. Which value makes the multiplication sentence true?

$$8.53 \times 6.3 = \underline{\quad}$$

A. 5,373.9
B. 53.739
C. 7.677
D. 537.39

SHOW YOUR WORK!

31. Sandy walked 1.5 miles each day for 7 days. What is the total number of miles that Sandy walked?

A. 10.5 days
B. 8.5 miles
C. 1.05 miles
D. 10.5 miles

SHOW YOUR WORK!

Think about it. Which operation can be used to find the total number of miles walked in 7 days? Remember, she walked the same number of miles each day.

32. Phillip and Jake divided 24.06 by 0.3. Phillip's quotient was 8.02, and Jake's quotient was 80.2. Whose answer is correct?

A. Phillip is correct.
B. They are both incorrect. The answer is 8.2.
C. Jake is correct.
D. They are both correct: 8.02 = 80.2.

SHOW YOUR WORK!

Test B   Name: _____

Directions: Read the word problem carefully. Select the best answer for each question.

Stella bought 13 puzzles for her grandchildren. Each puzzle cost $2.75. She gave the clerk $40.00. How much change did Stella get back?

33. Which operation would you use to solve the first step of the problem?

   A. addition

   B. multiplication

   C. subtraction

   D. division

> Stella bought 13 puzzles and each puzzle cost the same amount. Which operation should be used to find how much Stella spent *in all*? Choose the *best* answer.

34. Which equation could be used to do the first step of the problem?

   A. $40.00 − $2.75 = $37.25

   B. $2.75 + 13 = $15.75

   C. $2.75 × 13 = $35.75

   D. $40.00 + 2.75 = $42.75

35. What information is used in step two?

   A. The number of puzzles Stella bought.

   B. Who Stella bought the puzzles for.

   C. The total amount Stella spent on all the puzzles.

   D. How much money Stella spent for each puzzle.

36. What is the answer to the word problem?

   A. $2.75

   B. $75.75

   C. $44.25

   D. $4.25

SHOW YOUR WORK!

> The change that Stella gets back is the *difference* between what she paid and what she owed.

Test B **Name:** _____

Directions: Read each problem carefully and select the best answer.

37. Which value makes the number sentence true?

$(8 \times 4) - (42 \div 7) + 4^3 =$ ___

A. 42

B. 38

C. 33

D. 90

SHOW YOUR WORK!

Simplify inside parentheses first. Then, use the *order of operations*: exponents, multiplication and division (left to right), addition and subtraction (left to right).

38. Evaluate the expression for $y = 3$.

$55 + (y \times 6) - 9$

A. 174

B. 339

C. 64

D. 73

SHOW YOUR WORK!

Evaluate means to solve. Replace *y* with 3, remember to do what is in parentheses first, and then follow the *order of operations*.

39. Simplify.

$(3 \times 7) \times (10 - 3^2)$

A. 105

B. 21

C. 84

D. 201

SHOW YOUR WORK!

40. Which number sentence is true?

A. $72 \div 2^3 + (7 - 2) = 14$

B. $(8 + 9) \times (3 - 2) + 1 = 17$

C. $(36 \div 6) \times (3^2 - 5) = 6$

D. $(3 \times 9) - (4 + 2 + 3) = 21$

SHOW YOUR WORK!

Test B   Name: _____

Directions: Read each problem carefully and select the best answer.

41. Which value makes the number sentence true?

$$11 + [(3 \times 2^3) - (4 \times 5)] \times 3 = \text{\_\_\_\_}$$

A. 17

B. 1,620

C. 23

D. 45

SHOW YOUR WORK!

> Do the computation inside the parentheses first and then inside the brackets. Think: should you add 11 first or multiply by 3 first?

42. Simplify.

$$360 - [(12 \times 6) \times (16 \div 8)] + 5$$

A. 221

B. 216

C. 581

D. 149

SHOW YOUR WORK!

> Use the *order of operations:* Simplify inside parentheses first, then brackets, and finally do multiplication and division (from left to right), then addition and subtraction (from left to right).

43. Evaluate for *r* = 4.

$$[(6 \times r) - (4 + 9)] \times 7$$

A. 67

B. 203

C. 11

D. 77

SHOW YOUR WORK!

44. Simplify.

$$52 - 8 + [(25 \div 5) \times (36 \div 4)]$$

A. 58

B. 89

C. 49

D. 1,980

SHOW YOUR WORK!

Test B   Name: _____

Directions: Read each problem carefully and select the best answer.

45. Rename $\frac{2}{7}$ and $\frac{2}{3}$ to equivalent fractions with a common denominator.

   A. $\frac{2}{7}$ and $\frac{2}{7}$

   B. $\frac{2}{21}$ and $\frac{2}{21}$

   C. $\frac{6}{21}$ and $\frac{14}{21}$

   D. $\frac{3}{21}$ and $\frac{7}{21}$

SHOW YOUR WORK!

> Don't forget to rename the numerators too.

46. Samantha is working on the last problem of her math homework. She must find a common denominator and rename the fractions $\frac{5}{6}$ and $\frac{1}{4}$ before adding them. Which fractions will Samantha use to solve the problem?

   A. $\frac{2}{12}$ and $\frac{3}{12}$

   B. $\frac{5}{12}$ and $\frac{1}{12}$

   C. $\frac{5}{6}$ and $\frac{1}{6}$

   D. $\frac{10}{12}$ and $\frac{3}{12}$

SHOW YOUR WORK!

47. Rename $\frac{1}{2}$ and $\frac{2}{9}$ to equivalent fractions with a common denominator.

   A. $\frac{9}{18}$ and $\frac{2}{18}$

   B. $\frac{1}{18}$ and $\frac{2}{18}$

   C. $\frac{1}{2}$ and $\frac{2}{2}$

   D. $\frac{9}{18}$ and $\frac{4}{18}$

SHOW YOUR WORK!

> Check your work! Did you use a common multiple for the denominator?

48. Andrew walked $\frac{3}{8}$ of a mile from the train station to his office. He decided to take the bus home from his office. He walked $\frac{1}{4}$ of mile to the bus station. He wants to know which station is closer to his office. He will need to rename both fractions with a common denominator before comparing. Which fractions will Andrew use to find which station is closer to his office?

   A. $\frac{3}{12}$ and $\frac{1}{12}$

   B. $\frac{3}{8}$ and $\frac{2}{8}$

   C. $\frac{3}{8}$ and $\frac{1}{8}$

   D. $\frac{3}{8}$ and $\frac{4}{8}$

SHOW YOUR WORK!

Test B　　Name: _____

Directions: Read each problem carefully and select the best answer. Answers should be in simplest form.

49. Lily walked $\frac{4}{9}$ of a mile to her friend's house to play. Later, she walked $\frac{2}{6}$ of a mile to her grandma's house to spend the night. How many miles did she walk in all?

A. $\frac{1}{9}$ of a mile

B. $\frac{14}{18}$ of a mile

C. $\frac{7}{9}$ of a mile

D. $\frac{2}{5}$ of a mile

> **SHOW YOUR WORK!**

> *In all* is a clue phrase to help you choose which operation to use.

50. Chrissy combined $\frac{1}{2}$ cup of yogurt with $\frac{1}{3}$ cup of pineapple to make herself a pineapple smoothie. How much pineapple smoothie did she make?

A. $\frac{2}{5}$ cup

B. $\frac{1}{6}$ cup

C. $\frac{5}{6}$ cup

D. $\frac{10}{12}$ cup

> **SHOW YOUR WORK!**

51. Marie has a ribbon $\frac{7}{8}$ of a yard long. She plans to use $\frac{3}{6}$ of a yard of the ribbon on her art project. How much ribbon will be left over?

A. $\frac{11}{24}$ of a yard

B. $\frac{9}{24}$ of a yard

C. $\frac{33}{24}$ of a yard

D. $\frac{3}{8}$ of a yard

> **SHOW YOUR WORK!**

> Remember to subtract only the numerators and keep the common denominator the same.

52. In the South Street Short Shop, $\frac{1}{3}$ of the shorts are white and $\frac{1}{5}$ of the shorts are navy blue. What fraction of the shorts are either white or navy blue?

A. $\frac{8}{15}$

B. $\frac{2}{8}$

C. $\frac{2}{15}$

D. $\frac{6}{15}$

> **SHOW YOUR WORK!**

| Test B | Name: _____ |

Directions: Read each problem carefully and select the best answer. Answers should be in simplest form.

53. Julia sprinted $2\frac{3}{4}$ laps and then jogged $4\frac{1}{4}$ laps. How many more laps did she jog than sprint?

A. 7 laps

B. $1\frac{2}{4}$ laps

C. $1\frac{1}{2}$ laps

D. $2\frac{1}{2}$ laps

SHOW YOUR WORK!

54. Gary and Clayton work at a local doughnut shop every Saturday morning. Gary sold $5\frac{5}{6}$ dozen of chocolate doughnuts and Clayton sold $4\frac{2}{3}$ dozen of glazed doughnuts. How many doughnuts did they sell all together?

A. $9\frac{9}{6}$ dozen

B. $10\frac{3}{6}$ dozen

C. $10\frac{1}{2}$ dozen

D. $1\frac{1}{6}$ dozen

SHOW YOUR WORK!

Remember to simplify the fractional part of your answer and combine the whole numbers.

55. Sophia made $6\frac{2}{4}$ gallons of lemonade for the picnic. After lunch, $3\frac{2}{3}$ of the lemonade remained. How much lemonade did the picnic guests drink?

A. $2\frac{10}{12}$ gallons

B. $3\frac{1}{6}$ gallons

C. $10\frac{1}{6}$ gallons

D. $2\frac{5}{6}$ gallons

SHOW YOUR WORK!

To find the *difference* between the amount of lemonade Sophia made and the amount of lemonade that was left after the picnic, find a common denominator and rename one of the fractions.

56. Osvaldo went to the farmer's market to buy fruit. He bought $1\frac{3}{4}$ pounds of grapes and $1\frac{5}{8}$ pounds of strawberries. How many pounds of fruit did Osvaldo buy?

A. $2\frac{3}{8}$ pounds

B. $3\frac{3}{8}$ pounds

C. $2\frac{11}{8}$ pounds

D. $2\frac{8}{12}$ pounds

SHOW YOUR WORK!

Test B   Name: _____

Directions: Read each problem carefully and select the best answer. Answers should be in simplest form.

57. Find the product.

SHOW YOUR WORK!

A. $\frac{18}{35}$

B. $\frac{15}{42}$

C. $\frac{5}{14}$

D. $\frac{35}{18}$

• • • • • • • • • • • • • • •
Check your work; use only
multiplication to find the
product.
• • • • • • • • • • • • • • •

58. Multiply.

SHOW YOUR WORK!

A. $\frac{1}{4}$

B. $\frac{7}{40}$

C. $\frac{25}{16}$

D. $\frac{5}{20}$

59. Robert Hill High School held an election for class president. Only $\frac{3}{4}$ of the student body voted on election day. The winning candidate received $\frac{2}{3}$ of the total votes. What fraction of the student body voted for the winning candidate?

A. $\frac{6}{12}$ of the student body

B. $\frac{1}{2}$ of the student body

C. $\frac{1}{12}$ of the student body

D. $\frac{2}{4}$ of the student body

SHOW YOUR WORK!

60. Robert Hill High School has a great athletic department. $\frac{3}{5}$ of the students that attend Robert Hill High School play sports. $\frac{1}{3}$ of the students that play a sport participate in the basketball program. What fraction of students participates in the basketball program?

A. $\frac{3}{15}$ of the students

B. $\frac{14}{15}$ of the students

C. $\frac{4}{15}$ of the students

D. $\frac{1}{5}$ of the students

SHOW YOUR WORK!

• • • • • • • • • • • • • • •
Find $\frac{1}{3}$ *of* $\frac{3}{5}$.
• • • • • • • • • • • • • • •

Test B Name: _____

Directions: Read each problem carefully and select the best answer. Answers should be in simplest form.

61. Find the product.

$$32 \times \frac{2}{8}$$

A. $\frac{1}{128}$

B. 8

C. $\frac{64}{8}$

D. $\frac{2}{256}$

SHOW YOUR WORK!

62. On Sunday morning, Laura's family decided they wanted French toast with powdered sugar on it for breakfast. Laura's mom sprinkled $\frac{3}{4}$ of a 2-cup bag of powdered sugar on the toast. How much powdered sugar did Laura's mom use?

A. $\frac{6}{4}$ cups

B. $1\frac{2}{4}$ cups

C. $\frac{3}{8}$ cup

D. $1\frac{1}{2}$ cups

SHOW YOUR WORK!

Find $\frac{3}{4}$ of 2.

63. Find $\frac{3}{5}$ of 8.

A. $\frac{24}{5}$

B. $\frac{3}{40}$

C. $\frac{11}{5}$

D. $4\frac{4}{5}$

SHOW YOUR WORK!

64. Haruo has 15 customers on his paper route. His friend Juan has $\frac{2}{3}$ as many customers. How many customers does Juan have?

A. 15 customers

B. 10 customers

C. 3 customers

D. 30 customers

SHOW YOUR WORK!

Does your answer make sense? The number of customers that Juan has is only a fraction of the customers that Haruo has.

Test B Name: _____

Directions: Read each problem carefully and select the best answer.

73. Which measurement is equal to 150 mm?

   A. 15 cm

   B. 1 m

   C. 15 in.

   D. 1,500 cm

> **SHOW YOUR WORK!**

74. Which measurement is equal to 12 gal.?

   A. 48 pt.

   B. 24 qt.

   C. 64 pt.

   D. 48 qt.

> **SHOW YOUR WORK!**

> 1 gallon = 4 quarts and
> 1 quart = 2 pints.
> *Multiply* when converting
> from larger to smaller units.

75. Justin is going to visit his grandmother. His grandmother lives 14 miles away. How many yards is that?

   A. 125 yd.
       and 10 ft.

   B. 24,640 yd.

   C. 14,000 yd.

   D. 73,920 yd.

> **SHOW YOUR WORK!**

> 1 mile = 5,280 ft.
> or 1,760 yd.
>
> *Multiply* miles by yards per
> mile to find the total.

76. Mary Ann's new bike weighs 7,000 g. How many kg does Mary Ann's bike weigh?

   A. 70 kg

   B. 7,000 kg

   C. 7 kg

   D. 700 kg

> **SHOW YOUR WORK!**

> 1,000 grams = 1 kilogram.
> *Divide* when converting from
> smaller to larger units.

Test B   Name: _____

Directions: Read each problem carefully and select the best answer.

Use the grid to answer questions 77 and 78.

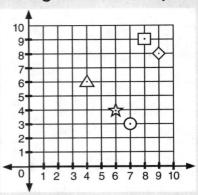

77. Which shape is located at (6,4) on the grid?

    A. diamond   **B.** circle   **C.** triangle   **D.** star

> Begin at 0, move to the right,
> then move up.

78. Which shape is located at (8,9) on the grid?

    A. triangle

    B. square

    C. circle

    D. diamond

Use the grid to answer questions 79 and 80.

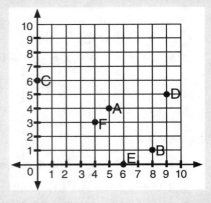

> Remember to count to the
> right until you are under *E*.
> Then, count up to *E*.

79. What is the ordered pair for point *E*?

    A. (6,0)   **B.** (0,6)   **C.** (9,5)   **D.** (4,3)

80. What is the ordered pair for point *A*?

    A. (8,1)   **B.** (4,3)   **C.** (5,4)   **D.** (0,6)

Test B   Name: _____

Directions: Read each problem carefully and select the best answer.

Use the information below to answer questions 81–84.

For every hockey game, the coach brought juice for the team. The values below show how many quarts of juice the team drank at each game.

$6\frac{1}{4}$, $10\frac{1}{2}$, $7\frac{1}{8}$, $9\frac{1}{2}$, $10\frac{1}{2}$, $6\frac{1}{4}$, $9\frac{1}{2}$, $10\frac{1}{2}$, $7\frac{1}{8}$, $6\frac{1}{4}$, $7\frac{1}{8}$, $6\frac{1}{4}$, $8\frac{3}{4}$, $9\frac{1}{2}$, $8\frac{3}{4}$,

$6\frac{1}{4}$, $8\frac{3}{4}$, $9\frac{1}{2}$, $10\frac{1}{2}$, $10\frac{1}{2}$, $7\frac{1}{8}$, $6\frac{1}{4}$

81. Which set of tally marks should be in the table for $6\frac{1}{4}$ quarts of juice?

A. TＨＨ

B. IIII

C. TＨＨ I

D. TＨＨ II

Number of Quarts	Tally	Frequency
$6\frac{1}{4}$		6
$7\frac{1}{8}$	IIII	4
$8\frac{3}{4}$	III	3
$9\frac{1}{2}$	IIII	4
$10\frac{1}{2}$	TＨＨ	5

82. What is the difference between the greatest and least number of quarts of juice drank at each game?

A. $16\frac{3}{4}$ quarts

B. $3\frac{1}{4}$ quarts

C. $4\frac{1}{4}$ quarts

D. $4\frac{1}{2}$ quarts

SHOW YOUR WORK!

Use the correct operation to find the *difference*.

83. How many Xs should be on the line plot to show the number of times the team drank $7\frac{1}{8}$ quarts of juice?

A. 6   C. 5

B. 3   D. 4

Each *X* represents one time that the coach brought juice to the team.

84. How many Xs would be on the line plot showing how many times the coach brought juice to a game?

A. 19   C. 17

B. 22   D. 16

Test B   Name: _____

Directions: Read each problem carefully and select the best answer.

85. What is the volume of this object in cubic units?

A. 29 cubic units

B. 15 cubic units

C. 20 cubic units

D. 25 cubic units

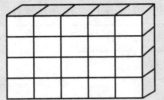

> Volume is calculated by counting *all* of the cubes that fit inside of a figure.

86. What is the volume of this object in cubic units?

A. 12 cubic units

B. 8 cubic units

C. 21 cubic units

D. 10 cubic units

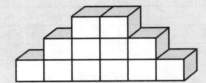

87. What is the volume of this object in cubic units?

A. 41 cubic units

B. 30 cubic units

C. 25 cubic units

D. 24 cubic units

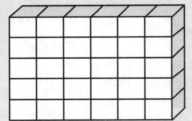

> Check your answer by multiplying length × width × height.

88. A large cube is made from 6 layers of small cubes. Each layer has 6 cubes. What is the total number of cubic units inside the large cube?

A. 36 units

B. 36 cubic units

C. 18 cubic units

D. 12 cubic units

SHOW YOUR WORK!

Test B | Name: _____

Directions: Read each problem carefully and select the best answer.

97. Which statement is true about two-dimensional figures?

A. All rectangles are squares.

B. All trapezoids are rectangles.

C. All rhombuses are rectangles.

D. All squares are rectangles.

> Remember, rectangles are not squares.

98. Which of the words below best describe this two-dimensional figure?

> Look closely at all of the answer choices so that you can choose the best one.

A. The figure is a parallelogram with four equal sides.

B. The figure is a rectangle with four equal sides.

C. The figure is rectangle with four right angles.

D. The figure is a square with four equal sides and four right angles.

99. Which statement is false about two-dimensional figures?

A. All trapezoids are quadrilaterals.

B. All squares are rectangles.

C. All rhombuses are rectangles.

D. All squares are rhombuses.

100. Which set of characteristics correctly describes the two-dimensional figure?

A. quadrilateral, parallelogram, rhombus

B. quadrilateral, parallelogram, rectangle

C. quadrilateral, rectangle, square

D. quadrilateral, parallelogram, trapezoid

Test C   Name: _____

Directions: Read each problem carefully and select the best answer.

1. 112 alien space ships invaded Earth. There were 25 aliens on each ship. How many aliens invaded Earth?

   A. 2,700 aliens
   B. 2,800 aliens
   C. 784 aliens
   D. 2,900 aliens

   SHOW YOUR WORK!

2. Multiply.

   | 309 × 29 |

   A. 8,961
   B. 8,861
   C. 3,399
   D. 8,981

   SHOW YOUR WORK!

3. Michael built a square shed in his backyard. One side of the shed is 16 feet long. What is the perimeter of the shed?

   A. 256 feet
   B. 44 feet
   C. 64 feet
   D. 66 feet

   SHOW YOUR WORK!

4. Find the product.

   | 96 × 72 |

   A. 6,812
   B. 864
   C. 6,922
   D. 6,912

   SHOW YOUR WORK!

Test C

Name: _____

Directions: Read each problem carefully and select the best answer.

5. The members of the middle school drama club have $168 to buy tickets to see a play downtown. Each ticket costs $14. How many tickets can they buy?

   A. 17 tickets

   B. 14 tickets

   C. 11 tickets

   D. 12 tickets

   SHOW YOUR WORK!

6. Find the quotient.

   84 ÷ 16

   A. 4 R20

   B. 6 R4

   C. 5 R4

   D. 5

   SHOW YOUR WORK!

7. The librarian has 196 new books. Each shelf in the library holds 14 books. How many shelves does the librarian need for the new books?

   A. 19 shelves

   B. 14 shelves

   C. 13 shelves

   D. 15 shelves

   SHOW YOUR WORK!

8. Divide.

   768 ÷ 35

   A. 21 R23

   B. 21 R33

   C. 22 R2

   D. 20 R68

   SHOW YOUR WORK!

Test C   Name: _____

Directions: Read each problem carefully and select the best answer.

9. What is $8{,}000 + 100 + 40 + 5 + \frac{5}{10} + \frac{3}{100} + \frac{9}{1{,}000}$ in standard form?

   A. 8,145.0539

   B. 80,145.539

   C. 81,045.539

   D. 8,145.539

   > **SHOW YOUR WORK!**

10. What is 37,281.4 in expanded form?

    > **SHOW YOUR WORK!**

    A. $3 \times 10{,}000 + 7 \times 1{,}000 + 2 \times 100 + 8 \times 10 + 1 \times 1 + 4 \times \frac{1}{100}$

    B. $3 \times 100{,}000 + 7 \times 1{,}000 + 2 \times 100 + 8 \times 10 + 1 \times 1 + 4 \times \frac{1}{10}$

    C. $3 \times 10{,}000 + 7 \times 1{,}000 + 2 \times 100 + 8 \times 10 + 1 \times 1 + 4 \times \frac{1}{10}$

    D. $3 \times 10{,}000 + 7 \times 1{,}000 + 2 \times 100 + 8 \times 10 + 1 \times 10 + 4 \times \frac{1}{10}$

11. Write *two and nine hundred sixty-eight thousandths* as a decimal.

    A. 2.0968

    B. 0.2968

    C. 2.968

    D. 2.00968

12. What is the word name for 67,033.94?

    A. sixty-seven thousand, thirty-three, and ninety-four hundredths

    B. sixty-seven thousand, thirty-three hundred, and ninety-four hundredths

    C. sixty-seven hundred, thirty-three, and ninety-four hundredths

    D. sixty-seven thousand, thirty-three, and ninety-four thousandths

Test C   Name: _____

Directions: Read each problem carefully and select the best answer.

13. Which fraction is equal to 3.027?

A. $3\frac{27}{10}$

B. $3\frac{27}{100}$

C. $\frac{327}{1,000}$

D. $3\frac{27}{1,000}$

14. Which decimal is equal to $6\frac{9}{10}$?

A. 6.009

B. 6.09

C. 0.69

D. 6.9

15. How many times less is the value of the digit *6* in 332,654 than the value of the digit *6* in 362,354?

A. 2 times

B. 10 times

C. 100 times

D. 1,000 times

SHOW YOUR WORK!

16. Which decimal is 100 times greater than 0.03?

A. 30.0

B. 3.0

C. 0.3

D. 0.0003

SHOW YOUR WORK!

Test C   Name: _____

Directions: Read each problem carefully and select the best answer.

17. Shirley drank 1.2 pints of juice. Jerry drank 1.02 pints of juice. Jim drank 1.002 pints of juice. Who drank the most juice?

    A. Jim drank the most juice.

    B. Shirley drank the most juice.

    C. Jerry drank the most juice.

    D. They all drank the same amount of juice.

    SHOW YOUR WORK!

18. Which list of decimals is in order from least to greatest?

    A. 2.562, 2.532, 2.522, 2.51

    B. 0.741, 0.75, 0.7, 0.8

    C. 0.1, 0.02, 0.003, 1.01

    D. 3.234, 3.43, 3.5, 3.567

19. Which number comes between 2.185 and 2.19?

    A. 2.189

    B. 2.183

    C. 2.191

    D. 2.18

    SHOW YOUR WORK!

20. Which number sentence is not true?

    A. 0.43 = 0.430

    B. 1.98 > 1.89

    C. 5.721 > 5.82

    D. 3.7 < 3.74

Test C	Name: _____

Directions: Read each problem carefully and select the best answer.

21. What is 238.928 rounded to the nearest tenth?
    A. 238.93
    B. 238.9
    C. 239.0
    D. 238.91

22. Tommy received $145.78 for his birthday. How much money did Tommy get for his birthday to the nearest hundred dollars?
    A. $100.00
    B. $200.00
    C. $146.00
    D. $145.80

23. Which number rounds to 15.372 when rounded to the nearest thousandth?
    A. 15.3711
    B. 15.3713
    C. 15.3726
    D. 15.3724

24. What is 153.552 rounded to the nearest ten?
    A. 153.6
    B. 154.0
    C. 150.0
    D. 200.0

Test C   Name: _____

Directions: Read each problem carefully and select the best answer.

25. Which value makes the subtraction sentence true?

| 53.3 – 29.58 = ___ |

SHOW YOUR WORK!

A. .2372

B. 82.88

C. 15.75

D. 23.72

26. Which value makes the addition sentence true?

| 16.78 + 75.4 = ___ |

SHOW YOUR WORK!

A. 92.18

B. 24.32

C. 2.432

D. 921.8

27. Josh and Kim took aluminum cans to the recycling center. Josh's cans weighed 93.4 g. Kim's cans weighed 92.92 g. How many grams did the cans weigh all together?

SHOW YOUR WORK!

A. 0.48 g

B. 102.26 g

C. 186.32 g

D. 18.632 g

28. The length of the auditorium in Robertsville School is 40.1 yd. The width of the auditorium is 36.37 yd. What is the difference between the length and the width of the auditorium?

SHOW YOUR WORK!

A. 3.87 yd.

B. 37.3 yd.

C. 3.73 yd.

D. 76.47 yd.

Test C　　Name: _____

Directions: Read each problem carefully and select the best answer.

29. Which value makes the division sentence true?

    | 46.86 ÷ 2.2 = ___ |

    SHOW YOUR WORK!

    A. 2.13
    B. 44.66
    C. 21.3
    D. 0.213

30. Which value makes the multiplication sentence true?

    | 7.08 × 8.7 = ___ |

    SHOW YOUR WORK!

    A. 6,159.6
    B. 10.620
    C. 615.96
    D. 61.596

31. Dyana ate 15.6 ounces of meat in 5.2 days. How many ounces of meat did she eat each day?

    A. 0.3 ounces
    B. 81.12 ounces
    C. 3.0 days
    D. 3.0 ounces

    SHOW YOUR WORK!

32. Brandon, his two brothers, his mom, and his dad went on a fishing trip. Each person had a fishing pole that weighed 602.65 grams. How much did the fishing poles weigh all together?

    A. 120.53 grams
    B. 3,013.25 grams
    C. 301.325 grams
    D. 2,410.60 grams

    SHOW YOUR WORK!

Test C	Name: _____

Directions: Read the word problem carefully. Select the best answer for each question.

Carl had a large bag of marbles that weighed 1.42 kilograms. He took 0.30 kilograms of marbles from the large bag and gave it to his brother. Then Carl equally separated the rest of the marbles into 4 smaller bags. How much does each of the smaller bags weigh?

33. What information do you need to find in step one before you can answer the question?

   A. The large bag weighed 1.42 kilograms.

   B. the number of marbles in the large bag and four small bags

   C. Carl gave his brother 0.30 kilograms of marbles.

   D. the weight of the marbles Carl had left after he gave some marbles to his brother

34. Which operation should you use to solve the first step of the problem?

   A. addition

   B. subtraction

   C. division

   D. multiplication

35. Which clue helps you decide what operation to use to solve step two of the problem?

   A. equally separated

   B. how much

   C. the smaller bags

   D. took 0.30 kilograms of marbles

36. What is the answer to the word problem?

   A. 0.28 bags of marbles

   B. 1.12 kilograms

   C. 0.28 kilograms

   D. 0.355 kilograms

SHOW YOUR WORK!

Test C   Name: _____

Directions: Read each problem carefully and select the best answer.

37. Which value makes the number sentence true?

$(5^2 + 5) \times (30 \div 10) - 2 =$ ____

SHOW YOUR WORK!

A. 43
B. 88
C. 90
D. 34

38. Which number sentence is not true?

A. $(2 + 3) \times (12 \div 4) + 3 = 45$
B. $4 + (45 \times 0) - 3 = 1$
C. $81 \div (3 + 2 + 4) \times 3 = 27$
D. $(7 \times 2) + (6 - 3) + 2 = 19$

SHOW YOUR WORK!

39. Simplify.

$(56 \div 8) \times (48 \div 8) + 10^2$

SHOW YOUR WORK!

A. 42
B. 62
C. 142
D. 54

40. Evaluate the expression for $n = 6$.

$(8 \times 3) \div (8 - n) + 6^2$

SHOW YOUR WORK!

A. 18
B. 39
C. 3
D. 48

Test C   Name: _____

Directions: Read each problem carefully and select the best answer.

41. Which value makes the number sentence true?

$$[95 - (12 \times 7)] + 9^3 = \underline{\quad}$$

A. 740

B. 1,310

C. 38

D. 729

SHOW YOUR WORK!

42. Simplify.

$$3 + [(6.31 \times 2.4) + (28.7 \div 4.1)] \times 2$$

A. 50.288

B. 44.288

C. 47.288

D. 25.144

SHOW YOUR WORK!

43. Evaluate for $w = 9$.

$$[(18 \div w) \times (8 + 3)] - 17$$

A. 2

B. 5

C. 82

D. 22

SHOW YOUR WORK!

44. Simplify.

$$246 - [(55 + 13) + (2^2 \times 6)]$$

A. 154

B. 202

C. 92

D. 166

SHOW YOUR WORK!

Test C   Name: _____

Directions: Read each problem carefully and select the best answer.

45. Nicole is planning to make a pillow and needs to know how much material to purchase. She needs 2 pieces of material $\frac{3}{8}$ foot long and 2 pieces of material $\frac{3}{4}$ foot long. To find the total amount of material to purchase, Nicole will need to rename the fractions with a common denominator and then add them together. Which fractions will Nicole use to determine the amount of material to purchase?

   A. $\frac{3}{8}$ and $\frac{3}{8}$

   B. $\frac{3}{8}$ and $\frac{2}{8}$

   C. $\frac{3}{8}$ and $\frac{6}{8}$

   D. $\frac{3}{8}$ and $\frac{4}{8}$

   SHOW YOUR WORK!

46. Rename $\frac{2}{3}$ and $\frac{5}{18}$ to equivalent fractions with a common denominator.

   A. $\frac{12}{18}$ and $\frac{5}{18}$

   B. $\frac{6}{18}$ and $\frac{5}{18}$

   C. $\frac{2}{18}$ and $\frac{5}{18}$

   D. $\frac{3}{18}$ and $\frac{5}{18}$

   SHOW YOUR WORK!

47. Mary drove $\frac{2}{3}$ of a mile to Wanda's house. Then Wanda drove Mary and herself $\frac{1}{2}$ of a mile to another friend's house for lunch. They want to know who drove the shortest distance. To compare the distances driven, they must find a common denominator and rename the fractions. Which fractions will they use to determine who drove the shortest distance?

   A. $\frac{2}{5}$ and $\frac{1}{5}$

   B. $\frac{2}{6}$ and $\frac{1}{6}$

   C. $\frac{2}{6}$ and $\frac{3}{6}$

   D. $\frac{4}{6}$ and $\frac{3}{6}$

   SHOW YOUR WORK!

48. Rename $\frac{5}{6}$ and $\frac{3}{4}$ to equivalent fractions with a common denominator.

   A. $\frac{2}{12}$ and $\frac{3}{12}$

   B. $\frac{10}{12}$ and $\frac{9}{12}$

   C. $\frac{5}{6}$ and $\frac{3}{6}$

   D. $\frac{5}{12}$ and $\frac{3}{12}$

   SHOW YOUR WORK!

Test C   Name: _____

Directions: Read each problem carefully and select the best answer. Answers should be in simplest form.

---

49. On Saturday, the corner ice-cream store had a special on ice-cream sundaes. $\frac{2}{4}$ of the sundaes sold were chocolate and $\frac{1}{3}$ of the sundaes sold were strawberry. What fraction of the sundaes sold were either strawberry or chocolate?

A. $\frac{10}{12}$ of the sundaes

B. $\frac{1}{6}$ of the sundaes

C. $\frac{5}{6}$ of the sundaes

D. $\frac{3}{7}$ of the sundaes

SHOW YOUR WORK!

---

50. John has $\frac{3}{7}$ of a yard of red rope and $\frac{6}{21}$ of a yard of blue rope. How much rope does he have all together?

A. $\frac{5}{7}$ of a yard

B. $\frac{15}{21}$ of a yard

C. $\frac{1}{7}$ of a yard

D. $\frac{9}{28}$ of a yard

SHOW YOUR WORK!

---

51. On Saturday, Nicholas bought $\frac{3}{4}$ gallon of gasoline for his lawn mower. On Sunday, he bought $\frac{2}{8}$ gallon of gasoline so he could mow the neighbor's yard. How much more gasoline did Nicholas buy on Saturday than on Sunday?

A. $\frac{4}{8}$ gallon

B. $\frac{2}{4}$ gallon

C. 1 gallon

D. $\frac{1}{2}$ gallon

SHOW YOUR WORK!

---

52. Margaret has $\frac{4}{6}$ of an ounce of grape jam. If Margaret puts $\frac{2}{8}$ of an ounce of grape jam on her toast, how much jam will she have left?

A. $\frac{3}{7}$ of an ounce

B. $\frac{5}{12}$ of an ounce

C. $\frac{10}{24}$ of an ounce

D. $\frac{11}{12}$ of an ounce

SHOW YOUR WORK!

Test C   Name: _____

Directions: Read each problem carefully and select the best answer. Answers should be in simplest form.

53. Andrew drives $21\frac{2}{5}$ miles to work each day and Michael drives $15\frac{1}{15}$ miles to work each day. How much farther does Andrew drive to work each day than Michael?

A. $6\frac{1}{3}$ miles

B. $6\frac{5}{15}$ miles

C. $7\frac{1}{3}$ miles

D. $6\frac{7}{15}$ miles

SHOW YOUR WORK!

54. Claudia used $5\frac{3}{5}$ yards of red fabric and $4\frac{1}{2}$ yards of green fabric to make decorations for the holiday. How much fabric did she use in all?

A. $9\frac{11}{10}$ yards

B. $10\frac{1}{10}$ yards

C. $1\frac{1}{10}$ yards

D. $9\frac{4}{7}$ yards

SHOW YOUR WORK!

55. Kako put $3\frac{4}{10}$ bags of fertilizer on the front lawn and $2\frac{2}{3}$ bags of fertilizer on the back lawn. How many bags of fertilizer did Kako put on the entire lawn?

A. $6\frac{2}{30}$ bags

B. $5\frac{6}{13}$ bags

C. $5\frac{1}{15}$ bags

D. $6\frac{1}{15}$ bags

SHOW YOUR WORK!

56. Angela ordered 7 pizzas for her party. After the party she had $3\frac{4}{12}$ pizzas left. How much pizza was eaten at the party?

A. $3\frac{8}{12}$ pizzas

B. $3\frac{4}{6}$ pizzas

C. $3\frac{2}{3}$ pizzas

D. $4\frac{2}{3}$ pizzas

SHOW YOUR WORK!

Test C **Name:** _____

Directions: Read each problem carefully and select the best answer. Answers should be in simplest form.

57. Find the product.

A. $\frac{1}{6}$

B. $\frac{1}{5}$

C. $\frac{6}{30}$

D. $\frac{5}{9}$

SHOW YOUR WORK!

58. Multiply.

A. $\frac{24}{36}$

B. $\frac{27}{32}$

C. $\frac{12}{18}$

D. $\frac{2}{3}$

SHOW YOUR WORK!

59. Wanda and Judy sold candles to raise money for the hurricane victims. Judy sold $\frac{1}{4}$ as many candles as Wanda. If Wanda sold $\frac{2}{3}$ of a box of candles, how many candles did Judy sell?

A. $\frac{2}{12}$ of a box

B. $\frac{11}{12}$ of a box

C. $\frac{1}{6}$ of a box

D. $\frac{3}{8}$ of a box

SHOW YOUR WORK!

60. Mary wants to make a small apple pie. The recipe calls for $\frac{5}{8}$ cup of apples. If she uses $\frac{1}{2}$ of the amount of apples the recipe calls for, how many cups of apples will she use?

A. $\frac{5}{16}$ cup

B. $\frac{6}{10}$ cup

C. $\frac{4}{5}$ cup

D. $1\frac{1}{8}$ cups

SHOW YOUR WORK!

Test C   Name: _____

Directions: Read each problem carefully and select the best answer. Answers should be in simplest form.

61. Find $\frac{2}{3}$ of 15.

A. $15\frac{2}{3}$

B. $\frac{2}{45}$

C. $\frac{30}{3}$

D. 10

SHOW YOUR WORK!

62. The Walker family made blueberry and blackberry preserves to share with the neighbors. They made 12 jars of blueberry preserves and $\frac{2}{3}$ as many jars of blackberry preserves. How many jars of blackberry preserves did they make?

A. 6 jars

B. $\frac{1}{18}$ jar

C. 8 jars

D. $\frac{24}{3}$ jars

SHOW YOUR WORK!

63. Find the product.

$$20 \times \frac{5}{8}$$

A. $\frac{1}{32}$

B. $3\frac{1}{8}$

C. $12\frac{1}{2}$

D. $12\frac{4}{8}$

SHOW YOUR WORK!

64. Samantha loves to bake chocolate chip cookies. She puts $\frac{3}{8}$ cup of chocolate chips in each batch of cookies she makes. Today she plans to bake 14 batches of chocolate chip cookies. How many cups of chocolate chips will she use?

A. $\frac{42}{8}$ cups

B. $5\frac{1}{4}$ cups

C. $2\frac{1}{8}$ cups

D. 5 cups

SHOW YOUR WORK!

Test C — Name: _____

Directions: Read each problem carefully and select the best answer. Answers should be in simplest form.

65. Divide.

$$3 \div \frac{5}{10}$$

A. $\frac{30}{5}$

B. $1\frac{1}{2}$

C. $\frac{1}{6}$

D. 6

SHOW YOUR WORK!

66. Jackie made $\frac{1}{2}$ gallon of punch. She needs to fill 6 glasses evenly with punch. How much punch should she put in each glass?

A. $\frac{1}{12}$ gallon

B. $\frac{1}{3}$ gallon

C. 3 gallons

D. 12 gallons

SHOW YOUR WORK!

67. Find the quotient.

$$\frac{3}{5} \div 3$$

A. $\frac{1}{3}$

B. $\frac{1}{5}$

C. $\frac{3}{15}$

D. $1\frac{4}{5}$

SHOW YOUR WORK!

68. Angie has $\frac{3}{4}$ of a meatloaf left over from dinner. She wants to divide it evenly among four family members for lunch. How much meatloaf will each family member receive?

A. 3 pieces of meatloaf

B. $\frac{1}{3}$ of the meatloaf

C. $\frac{3}{16}$ of the meatloaf

D. $5\frac{1}{3}$ pieces of meatloaf

SHOW YOUR WORK!

Test C   Name: _____

Directions: Read each problem carefully and select the best answer. Answers should be in simplest form.

69. The baker has a $\frac{1}{2}$ pound block of butter. He wants to cut it into 3 equal parts. How much will each of the three equal parts weigh?

A. $1\frac{1}{2}$ pounds

B. $\frac{2}{3}$ pound

C. $\frac{1}{6}$ pound

D. 6 pounds

> **SHOW YOUR WORK!**

70. The art teacher has a bucket of clay that is $\frac{4}{6}$ full. She wants to divide the clay evenly between 5 classrooms. How much clay will each classroom receive?

A. $\frac{4}{30}$ bucket

B. $\frac{2}{15}$ bucket

C. $3\frac{1}{3}$ buckets

D. $\frac{3}{10}$ bucket

> **SHOW YOUR WORK!**

71. The chef at an Italian restaurant has 4 bags of flour to make pizza. He uses $\frac{1}{3}$ of the flour for one pizza. How much flour does he use to make one pizza?

A. 12 bags

B. $\frac{4}{3}$ bag

C. $1\frac{1}{2}$ bags

D. $1\frac{1}{3}$ bags

> **SHOW YOUR WORK!**

72. Julia swam 5 laps in the pool. Nick swam $\frac{5}{8}$ as many laps. How many laps did Nick swim?

A. $\frac{25}{8}$ laps

B. $3\frac{1}{8}$ laps

C. $\frac{1}{8}$ lap

D. 8 laps

> **SHOW YOUR WORK!**

Test C Name: _____

Directions: Read each problem carefully and select the best answer.

73. Which measurement is equal to 8,000 pounds?

A. 4 kg

B. 4 T

C. 32,000 oz.

D. 8 T

SHOW YOUR WORK!

74. Which measurement is equal to 141 feet?

A. 423 yd.

B. 47 cm

C. 47 yd.

D. 846 in.

SHOW YOUR WORK!

75. Jonathan's backyard is 24 meters long. How many centimeters long is his backyard?

A. 2,400 cm

B. 240 cm

C. 24,000 cm

D. 1,200 cm

SHOW YOUR WORK!

76. The store has 6 L of lemon soda to sell. How many mL of lemon soda does the store have?

A. 3,000 mL

B. 600 mL

C. 12,000 mL

D. 6,000 mL

SHOW YOUR WORK!

Test C   Name: _____

Directions: Read each problem carefully and select the best answer.

77. Which shape is located at (2,7) on the grid?

A. diamond

B. circle

C. triangle

D. star

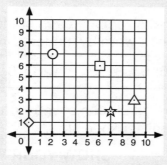

78. Which shape is located at (9,3) on the grid?

A. star

B. square

C. triangle

D. diamond

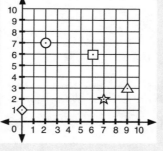

79. What is the ordered pair for point *C*?

A. (1,4)

B. (3,6)

C. (8,4)

D. (7,1)

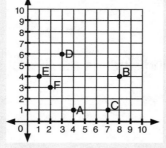

80. What is the ordered pair for point *E*?

A. (4,1)

B. (1,4)

C. (2,3)

D. (3,6)

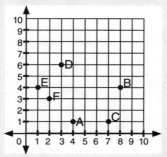

Test C   Name: _____

Directions: Read each problem carefully and select the best answer.

Use the information below to answer questions 81–84.

Mrs. Cook's class took a survey to find out what size shoe each student in the class wore. The values below show the sizes of shoes worn by students in the class.

$7\frac{1}{2}, 8\frac{1}{2}, 6\frac{1}{2}, 7, 10\frac{1}{2}, 6\frac{1}{2}, 8\frac{1}{2}, 10\frac{1}{2}, 8\frac{1}{2}, 6\frac{1}{2}, 7, 6, 9\frac{1}{2}, 8\frac{1}{2}, 5\frac{1}{2}, 7\frac{1}{2}, 8\frac{1}{2}, 6\frac{1}{2}, 9\frac{1}{2}, 9, 7\frac{1}{2}$

81. What is the difference between the number of students who wore the largest shoe size and the student wearing the smallest shoe size?

   A. 5 students

   B. 3 students

   C. 2 students

   D. 1 student

SHOW YOUR WORK!

82. How many students wore a shoe size larger than $7\frac{1}{2}$?

   A. 10 students

   B. 5 students

   C. 13 students

   D. 8 student

83. How many Xs should be on a line plot to indicate the number of students that wore size $6\frac{1}{2}$?

   A. 5

   B. 4

   C. 3

   D. 6

84. How many students took the survey?

   A. 22 students

   B. 19 students

   C. 21 students

   D. 20 students

Test C   Name: _____

Directions: Read each problem carefully and select the best answer.

85. What is the volume of this object in cubic units?

   A. 15 units
   B. 18 cubic units
   C. 23 cubic units
   D. 15 cubic units

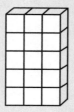

SHOW YOUR WORK!

86. What is the volume of this object in cubic units?

   A. 15 cubic units
   B. 56 cubic units
   C. 48 cubic units
   D. 71 cubic units

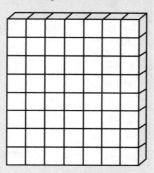

SHOW YOUR WORK!

87. What is the volume of this object in cubic units?

   A. 10 cubic units
   B. 18 cubic units
   C. 7 cubic units
   D. 8 cubic units

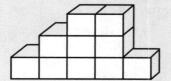

SHOW YOUR WORK!

88. There are 14 cubes in each layer and there are 3 layers. What is the total number of cubic units in this figure?

   A. 28 cubic units
   B. 17 cubic units
   C. 42 cubic units
   D. 42 units

SHOW YOUR WORK!

Test C	Name: _____

Directions: Read each problem carefully and select the best answer.

89. What is the volume of the rectangular prism?

    A. 17 ft.³

    B. 108 ft.³

    C. 54 ft.³

    D. 18 ft.³

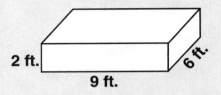

SHOW YOUR WORK!

90. What is the volume of this figure?

    A. 271 m²

    B. 271 m³

    C. 271 m

    D. 231 m³

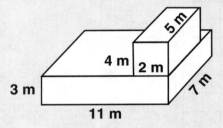

SHOW YOUR WORK!

91. What is the volume of this figure?

    A. 360 cm³

    B. 34 cm³

    C. 310 cm³

    D. 410 cm³

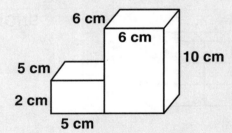

SHOW YOUR WORK!

92. Betty Ann has a stack of books that has a length of 7 in., a width of 6 in., and a height of 24 in. What is the volume of the stack of books?

    A. 144 in.³

    B. 42 in.³

    C. 1,008 in.³

    D. 37 in.³

SHOW YOUR WORK!

Test C   Name: _____

Directions: Read each problem carefully and select the best answer. Answers should be in simplest form.

93. Farmer Vic set aside a rectangular piece of land measuring $12\frac{1}{2}$ feet long and $10\frac{4}{5}$ feet wide to grow vegetables. What is the area of the land Farmer Vic set aside for growing vegetables?

SHOW YOUR WORK!

- A. $\frac{135}{1}$ sq. feet
- B. 135 sq. feet
- C. $120\frac{2}{5}$ sq. feet
- D. $\frac{1,350}{10}$ sq. feet

94. Find the area of the rectangle.

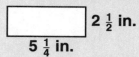 $2\frac{1}{2}$ in.

$5\frac{1}{4}$ in.

SHOW YOUR WORK!

- A. $10\frac{1}{8}$ sq. inches
- B. $4\frac{1}{3}$ sq. feet
- C. $\frac{105}{8}$ sq. inches
- D. $13\frac{1}{8}$ sq. inches

95. Nicole wants to hang wallpaper on one wall in her bedroom. She needs to know the area of the wall to buy the wallpaper. The wall is $7\frac{1}{2}$ feet wide and $10\frac{2}{3}$ feet high. What is the area of the wall?

- A. $70\frac{1}{3}$ sq. feet
- B. $\frac{480}{6}$ sq. feet
- C. 80 sq. feet
- D. $\frac{80}{1}$ sq. feet

SHOW YOUR WORK!

96. Find the area of the rectangle.

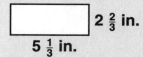 $2\frac{2}{3}$ in.

$5\frac{1}{3}$ in.

- A. $14\frac{2}{9}$ sq. feet
- B. $\frac{128}{9}$ sq. feet
- C. $10\frac{2}{9}$ sq. feet
- D. 4 sq. feet

SHOW YOUR WORK!

Test C   **Name:** _____

Directions: Read each problem carefully and select the best answer.

97. Which statement describes how a rhombus and a square are alike?

   A. A rhombus and a square both have four right angles.

   B. A rhombus and a square both have sides of equal length.

   C. A rhombus and a square are both rectangles.

   D. none of the above

98. Which set of names can be used to describe the two-dimensional figure?

   A. quadrilateral, rhombus

   B. quadrilateral, rectangle

   C. quadrilateral, square

   D. quadrilateral, trapezoid

99. Which quadrilateral is not a parallelogram and never has all sides of equal length?

   A. rhombus

   B. rectangle

   C. square

   D. trapezoid

100. Which of the statements below *best* describes this two-dimensional figure?

   A. The figure is a parallelogram with no right angles.

   B. The figure is a rectangle with four sides of equal length.

   C. The figure is a rectangle with four right angles.

   D. The figure is a square with four sides of equal length and four right angles.

Master Answer Sheet

Answers for Test A (pages 10–34)

1. C	11. B	21. B	31. D	41. B	51. D	61. A	71. B	81. D	91. D
2. B	12. A	22. B	32. B	42. D	52. C	62. D	72. D	82. B	92. C
3. D	13. D	23. B	33. C	43. C	53. D	63. C	73. C	83. C	93. A
4. A	14. C	24. D	34. D	44. D	54. C	64. D	74. B	84. A	94. C
5. D	15. D	25. D	35. B	45. D	55. B	65. C	75. D	85. B	95. D
6. B	16. B	26. B	36. A	46. C	56. C	66. D	76. A	86. D	96. B
7. D	17. B	27. A	37. C	47. C	57. D	67. B	77. C	87. A	97. B
8. B	18. D	28. C	38. A	48. B	58. B	68. D	78. A	88. C	98. B
9. C	19. C	29. C	39. D	49. B	59. C	69. B	79. D	89. C	99. D
10. D	20. A	30. A	40. B	50. A	60. C	70. C	80. B	90. B	100. C

Answers for Test B (pages 35–59)

1. B	11. C	21. A	31. D	41. C	51. D	61. B	71. C	81. C	91. C
2. D	12. C	22. D	32. C	42. A	52. A	62. D	72. A	82. C	92. A
3. C	13. C	23. B	33. B	43. D	53. C	63. D	73. A	83. D	93. B
4. A	14. B	24. B	34. C	44. B	54. C	64. B	74. D	84. B	94. C
5. D	15. B	25. A	35. C	45. C	55. D	65. B	75. B	85. C	95. D
6. C	16. C	26. C	36. D	46. D	56. B	66. C	76. C	86. A	96. A
7. B	17. A	27. B	37. D	47. D	57. C	67. C	77. D	87. B	97. D
8. B	18. C	28. D	38. C	48. B	58. A	68. A	78. B	88. B	98. D
9. B	19. D	29. A	39. B	49. C	59. B	69. A	79. A	89. A	99. C
10. A	20. B	30. B	40. A	50. C	60. D	70. D	80. C	90. D	100. B

Answers for Test C (pages 60–84)

1. B	11. C	21. B	31. D	41. A	51. D	61. D	71. D	81. D	91. D
2. A	12. A	22. A	32. B	42. C	52. B	62. C	72. B	82. A	92. C
3. C	13. D	23. D	33. D	43. B	53. A	63. C	73. B	83. B	93. B
4. D	14. D	24. C	34. B	44. A	54. B	64. B	74. C	84. C	94. D
5. D	15. C	25. D	35. A	45. C	55. D	65. D	75. A	85. D	95. C
6. C	16. B	26. A	36. C	46. A	56. C	66. A	76. D	86. B	96. A
7. B	17. B	27. C	37. B	47. D	57. B	67. B	77. B	87. A	97. B
8. B	18. D	28. C	38. A	48. B	58. D	68. C	78. C	88. C	98. D
9. D	19. A	29. C	39. C	49. C	59. C	69. C	79. D	89. B	99. D
10. C	20. C	30. D	40. D	50. A	60. A	70. B	80. B	90. B	100. D

Explanations for Test A Answers

Multiplying Multi-digit Numbers (page 10)

1. **Correct Answer: C**
   Follow steps 1–6. 1. Write 62 under 64. **2.** Multiply 64 by 2 ones to get 128. **3.** Write the partial product (128). **4.** Multiply 64 by 6 tens to get 3,840 (remember to regroup). **5.** Write the partial product (3,840). **6.** Add the partial products: $128 + 3,840 = 3,968$.
   Incorrect Answers:
   A. In step 4, 64 was multiplied by 6 ones instead of by 6 tens. (The 6 in 64 is worth 6 tens.)
   B. An error occurred when adding the partial products.
   D. An error occurred when adding the partial products.

2. **Correct Answer: B**
   13 boxes of dressing × 25 packets per box = 325 packets of dressing used each day.
   Incorrect Answers:
   A. An extra *5* was inserted into the answer.
   C. 13 was multiplied by 2 ones instead of by 2 tens. (The 2 in 25 is worth 2 tens.)
   D. An error occurred when adding the partial products.

3. **Correct Answer: D**
   Follow steps 1–6. 1. Write 32 under 632.
   2. Multiply 632 by 2 ones to get 1,264.
   3. Write the partial product (1,264).
   4. Multiply 632 by 3 tens to get 18,960 (remember to regroup).
   5. Write the partial product (18,960).
   6. Add the partial products: $1,264 + 18,960 = 20,224$.
   Incorrect Answers:
   A. An error occurred in the hundreds column when adding the partial products.
   B. An error occurred when regrouping to add the ten-thousands column of the partial products.
   C. 632 was multiplied by 3 ones instead of by 3 tens. (The 3 in 32 is worth 3 tens.)

4. **Correct Answer: A**
   124 tennis balls per carton × 12 cartons = 1,488 tennis balls
   Incorrect Answers:
   B. An error occurred in the thousands place when adding the partial products.
   C. 124 was multiplied by 1 one instead of by 1 ten. (The 1 in 12 is worth 1 ten.)
   D. An error occurred when adding the partial products.

Dividing by Two-digit Divisors (page 11)

5. **Correct Answer: D**
   The divisor (19) is greater than the first digit in the dividend (7), so divide 19 into the first two digits (79) of the dividend. *DIVIDE:* $79 ÷ 19 = 4$. (Think $80 ÷ 20$.) Write 4 in the quotient above 9. *MULTIPLY:* $4 × 19 = 76$. *SUBTRACT:* $79 − 76 = 3$. The *remainder* is 3. The *quotient* is 4 R3.
   Incorrect Answers:
   A. A subtraction error occurred: $(79 − 76 ≠ 5)$.
   B. A division error occurred in the first step: 19 does not go into 79 five times.
   C. The remainder (22) cannot be greater than the divisor (19).

6. **Correct Answer: B**
   Divide the total amount of money raised by the number of students to find out how much money each student raised:
   $666 ÷ 74 = 9$.

Incorrect Answers:
   A. $74 × 7 = 518$, leaving room for 74 to go into 666 two more times.
   C. $74 × 8 = 592$, leaving room for 74 to go into 666 one more time.
   D. $74 × 10 = 740$; this is greater than 666.

7. **Correct Answer: D**
   The divisor (45) is greater than the first digit in the dividend (9), so divide 45 into the first two digits (94). *DIVIDE:* $94 ÷ 45 = 2$. Write 2 in the quotient above 4. *MULTIPLY* $2 × 45 = 90$. *SUBTRACT:* $94 − 90 = 4$. *BRING DOWN:* the 5 from the ones column of the dividend to form the number 45. *DIVIDE:* $45 ÷ 45 = 1$. Write 1 in the quotient above 5. *MULTIPLY:* $1 × 45 = 45$. *SUBTRACT:* $45 − 45 = 0$. The quotient is 21.
   Incorrect Answers:
   A. A division error occurred when dividing 45 by 45: $45 ÷ 45 ≠ 5$ because $5 × 45 = 225$ and 225 is greater than 45.
   B. The remainder must be less than the divisor.
   C. An error occurred when subtracting $45 − 45$ in the last step.

8. **Correct Answer: B**
   68 slices of pizza needed for the party ÷ 8 slices per pizza = 8 R4. The quotient means that 8 whole pizzas are needed, plus 4 additional slices. In order to get the 4 additional slices that are needed, a whole pizza must be ordered:
   8 pizzas + 1 pizza = 9 pizzas.
   Incorrect Answers:
   A. 8 pizzas will only provide 64 slices; the remainder 4 was not factored into the final answer.
   C. 7 pizzas × 8 slices per pizza = 56 slices; this is not enough pizza.
   D. 12 pizzas × 8 slices per pizza = 96 slices; this is too much pizza.

Reading and Writing Decimals to Thousandths (page 12)

9. **Correct Answer: C**
   $4,328.12 = 4,000 + 300 + 20 + 8 + 0.1 + 0.02$
   Incorrect Answers:
   A. 4,328.3
   B. 938
   D. 4,580.12

10. **Correct Answer: D**
    $600,000 + 70,000 + 9,000 + 300 + 80 + 7 + 0.3 + 0.07 + 0.005 = 679,387.375$
    Incorrect Answers:
    A. 9 is missing from the thousands place.
    B. .0375 represents $\frac{3}{100} + \frac{7}{1,000} + \frac{5}{10,000}$.
    C. 7 is missing from the hundredths place and 5 is in the hundredths place instead of the thousandths place.

11. **Correct Answer: B**
    3,702.94 = three *thousand*, seven *hundred*, two (*ones*) and ninety-four *hundredths*
    Incorrect Answers:
    A. *seventy-two hundred* = 7,200.
    $3,000 + 7,200 + 0.94 = 10,200.94$
    C. 3,702.094
    D. *ninety-four hundreds* = 9,400.
    $3,000 + 702 + 9,400 = 13,102$

Explanations for Test A Answers *(cont.)*

12. Correct Answer: A

There is no *and* in the number name and the label is thousand*ths*, so all digits are written after the decimal point.
Incorrect Answers:
- **B.** This is three *and* seventy-six thousandths.
- **C.** This is three hundred seventy-six.
- **D.** This is three hundred seventy-six ten thousandths.

Interpreting Place Value *(page 13)*

13. Correct Answer: D

2.486 = two and four hundred eighty-six thousandths
Incorrect Answers:
- **A.** two and four hundred eighty-six hundredths = 2 + 4.86 = 6.86
- **B.** two thousand four hundred eighty-six hundredths = 24.86
- **C.** two and four hundred eighty-six tenths = 2 + 48.6 = 50.6

14. Correct Answer: C

$\frac{7}{100}$ = seven hundredths = 0.07
Incorrect Answers:
- **A.** $0.007 = \frac{7}{1,000}$
- **B.** $0.7 = \frac{7}{10}$
- **D.** $0.700 = \frac{700}{1,000} = \frac{7}{10}$

15. Correct Answer: D

In 930,625 the 9 is worth nine hundred thousands or 900,000. In 310,925 the 9 is worth nine hundreds or 900. 900,000 = *1,000* × 900, so 900,000 is 1,000 times greater than 900.
Incorrect Answers:
- **A.** The 9 in 930,625 is three *places* to the left of the 9 in 310,925, but each place value is worth *10 times* the place value to its right.
- **B.** The value of the number 100 times greater than 900 is 90,000: 900 × 100 ≠ 900,000.
- **C.** The value of the number 100,000 times greater than 900 is 90,000,000: 900 × 100,000 ≠ 900,000.

16. Correct Answer: B

$\frac{1}{10}$ of $0.4 = \frac{1}{10} \times 0.4 = 0.1 \times 0.4 = 0.04$
Incorrect Answers:
- **A.** 4 is 10 times 0.4.
- **C.** 4.1 is $\frac{1}{10}$ plus 4.0.
- **D.** 0.004 is $\frac{1}{100}$ of 0.4.

Comparing Decimals to Thousandths *(page 14)*

17. Correct Answer: B

2.4<u>3</u> > 2.4<u>2</u>1
Incorrect Answers:
- **A.** 2.4<u>3</u> < 2.4<u>5</u>
- **C.** 2.4<u>3</u> < 2.<u>9</u>
- **D.** 2.43 = 2.43

18. Correct Answer: D

8.625, 8.627, 8.70<u>0</u>, 8.711 are in order from least to greatest: 625 < 627 < 700 < 711.
Incorrect Answers:
- **A.** 4.96 is the greatest decimal, not the least. The order should be 4.872, 4.876, 4.878, 4.96.
- **B.** 1.75, 1.34, 1.29, 0.9 are in order from greatest to least, not least to greatest.
- **C.** 3.5 is the least decimal, not the greatest. The order should be 3.5, 3.512, 3.52, 3.55.

19. Correct Answer: C

6.754 > 6.77 is not true: 6.7<u>5</u>4 < 6.7<u>7</u>.
Incorrect Answers:
- **A.** 3.8<u>1</u> > 3.8<u>0</u>1 is true.
- **B.** 0.019 = 0.019 is true.
- **D.** 5.<u>2</u>56 < 5.<u>5</u>26 is true.

20. Correct Answer: A

Marie ran 3.6 miles and Frank ran 3.60 miles, so they both ran the same number of miles: 3.6<u>0</u> = 3.60. They ran more than Eddie: 3.<u>6</u>0 > 3.<u>0</u>6.
Incorrect Answers:
- **B.** Marie ran the same number of miles as Frank, so she alone did not run the greatest number of miles.
- **C.** Eddie ran the least number of miles.
- **D.** Frank ran the same number of miles as Marie, so he alone did not run the greatest number of miles.

Rounding Decimals *(page 15)*

21. Correct Answer: B

<u>7</u>,603.6819 ≈ 8,000. Since the digit to the right of the thousands place (6) is greater than 5, round up.
Incorrect Answers:
- **A.** 7,603.68 was rounded to the nearest hundredth, not the nearest thousand.
- **C.** 7,000 was incorrectly rounded down instead of up.
- **D.** 7,603.682 was rounded to the nearest thousandth, not the nearest thousand.

22. Correct Answer: B

44.<u>2</u>09 ≈ 44.2. Since the digit to the right of the tenths place (0) is less than 5, round down.
Incorrect Answers:
- **A.** 44.3 was incorrectly rounded up instead of down.
- **C.** 44.21 was rounded to the nearest hundredth instead of the nearest tenth.
- **D.** 40.0 was rounded to the nearest ten instead of the nearest tenth.

23. Correct Answer: B

$15.54 is the only given amount that rounds to $15.50.
Incorrect Answers:
- **A.** $15.44 rounds to $15.40.
- **C.** $15.55 rounds to $15.60.
- **D.** Marco has *about* $15.50 in his pocket, so he does not have exactly $15.50.

24. Correct Answer: D

$1<u>5</u>.56 ≈ $16.00. Since the digit to the right of the one-dollar place is 5, round up.
Incorrect Answers:
- **A.** $15.60 is $15.56 rounded to the nearest tenth.
- **B.** $20.00 is $15.56 rounded to the nearest ten.
- **C.** $15.56 was incorrectly rounded down instead of up.

Explanations for Test A Answers *(cont.)*

Adding and Subtracting Decimals *(page 16)*

25. Correct Answer: D
Align the decimal points to add:
```
  14.4
+ 3.58
 17.98
```
Incorrect Answers:
A. The decimal points were not aligned before adding.
B. The decimal points were not aligned before adding.
C. The decimal point is not in the correct place.

26. Correct Answer: B
Align the decimal points to subtract, and fill in any blank places at the end of the number with 0:
```
  8.50
- 6.27
  2.23
```
Incorrect Answers:
A. A zero was not added to 8.5 before subtracting; the 7 from 6.27 was just brought down.
C. The decimal points were not aligned before subtracting; instead, the numbers were aligned flush right.
D. The decimal points were not aligned before subtracting; instead, the numbers were aligned flush right.

27. Correct Answer: A
Align the decimal points to subtract:
```
  85.25
- 82.35
   2.90
```
Incorrect Answers:
B. The decimals were added instead of subtracted.
C. After regrouping from the ones place to the tenths place, the 5 in the ones place was not reduced to 4.
D. The decimal is not in the correct place.

28. Correct Answer: C
Align the decimal points to add:
```
  2.5
+ 3.81
  6.31
```
Incorrect Answers:
A. 2.5 km and 3.81 km were subtracted instead of added.
B. The decimal is not in the correct place.
D. The decimals were not aligned before adding; instead the numbers were aligned flush right.

Multiplying and Dividing Decimals *(page 17)*

29. Correct Answer: C
Follow steps 1–6 to multiply, ignoring decimal points until the last step: 1. Multiply 52 by 7. **2.** Write the partial product (364). **3.** Multiply 52 by 3. **4.** Write the partial product, including a place holder (1560). **5.** Add the partial products (1924). **6.** Place the decimal point in the final product (19.24).
Incorrect Answers:
A. The decimal point is not in the correct place.
B. 8.9 was calculated by adding instead of multiplying.
D. The decimal point is not in the correct place.

30. Correct Answer: A
Move the decimal point in the divisor to make a whole number, and move the decimal point in the dividend the same number of places. 0.5 becomes 5 and 6.25 becomes 62.5.
```
        12.5
    5 )62.5
      -5
       12
      -10
        2 5
       -2 5
          0
```
Incorrect Answers:
B. The decimal point is not in the correct place.
C. The decimal point is not in the correct place.
D. The dividend and the divisor were reversed: $0.5 \div 6.25 = 0.08$.

31. Correct Answer: D
Divide 9.36 minutes by 0.2 minute intervals for each jump to see how many jumps made up the 9.36 minutes: $9.36 \div 0.2 = 46.8$.
Incorrect Answers:
A. The numbers were multiplied instead of divided.
B. The decimal point is not in the correct place.
C. The decimal point is not in the correct place.

32. Correct Answer: B
Multiply to find the total cost: $0.48 per bag × 6 bags = $2.88.
Incorrect Answers:
A. $0.08 was calculated by dividing instead of multiplying.
C. $0.54 was calculated by incorrectly adding (decimal points were not lined up) $0.48 + 6 bags, instead of multiplying.
D. $0.42 was calculated by incorrectly subtracting (decimal points were not lined up) $0.48 – 6 bags, instead of multiplying.

Multiple-step Problems with Decimals *(page 18)*

33. Correct Answer: C
The total number of pints of berries Carol has must be known in order to find how much she has left after some are used.
Incorrect Answers:
A. The amount of all the berries used needs to be known, not just the amount of strawberries.
B. It does not matter how much of each type of berry is used; the question asks about the total amount of berries left.
D. What Carol does with the rest of the berries is irrelevant information.

34. Correct Answer: D
5.36 pints of strawberries + 4.82 pints of blueberries + 3.49 pints of raspberries = 13.67 pints of berries
Incorrect Answers:
A. 16.92 pints of berries was calculated by adding what Carol used to make the fruit salad (3.25) to the total amount of berries (13.67). Step one requires finding the total amount of berries available.
B. 10.18 pints is the amount of strawberries and blueberries Carol had; it does not include the amount of raspberries she had.
C. 13.43 pints of berries was calculated by adding the numbers of pints of strawberries and blueberries to the number of pints that Carol used (3.25) instead of to the number of pints of raspberries she had (3.49).

Explanations for Test A Answers *(cont.)*

35. Correct Answer: B
Have left is a clue to find the difference; the operation is subtraction.
Incorrect Answers:
A. *How many pints of berries* does not give a clue to what operation to use.
C. *Does Carol have* does not give a clue to what operation to use.
D. *Make a fruit salad* does not give a clue to what operation to use.

36. Correct Answer: A
13.67 pints of berries – 3.25 pints used = 10.42 pints of berries left over
Incorrect Answers:
B. 16.92 pints of berries is the sum of all the numbers given in the problem.
C. In 104.2 pints of berries, the decimal is not in the correct place.
D. *Pints of fruit salad* is the wrong label.

Simplifying Expressions (page 19)

37. Correct Answer: C
$(6 \times 5) + (10 - 3) = 30 + 7 = 37$
Incorrect Answers:
A. 210 was calculated by multiplying 30×7 instead of adding $30 + 7$.
B. 18 was calculated by adding $6 + 5$ instead of multiplying.
D. 30 is the product of 6×5; it does not include *+ (10 – 3)*.

38. Correct Answer: A
$2^3 \times (9 + 7) = 8 \times 16 = 128$
Incorrect Answers:
B. 2^3 was incorrectly simplified to 6 instead of 8: $6 \times (9 + 7) = 6 \times 16 = 96$.
C. 2^3 was incorrectly simplified to 4 instead of 8: $4 \times (9 + 7) = 4 \times 16 = 64$.
D. The parentheses step in the order of operations was ignored: $2^3 \times 9 + 7 = 8 \times 9 + 7 = 79$.

39. Correct Answer: D
$(24 \div 6) \times 3 + 5 = 4 \times 3 + 5 = 12 + 5 = 17$
Incorrect Answers:
A. The order of operations was not followed: 27 was calculated by adding $4 + 5$ then multiplying by 3 instead of multiplying 4×3 then adding the product to 5.
B. The order of operations was not followed: 32 was calculated by adding $3 + 5$ before multiplying 4×3.
C. 12 was calculated by dividing $24 \div 6$ and then multiplying by 3. 5 was not added to the answer.

40. Correct Answer: B
Replace *n* with 4: $(7 + 2) \div (3 \times 1) + 4 = 9 \div 3 + 4 = 3 + 4 = 7$.
Incorrect Answers:
A. $(4 + 3) \times (5 - 3) = 7 \times 2 = 14 \neq 9$
C. $(6 \times 3) + 4 + 3^2 = 18 + 4 + 9 = 31 \neq 28$
D. $4 + (63 \div 9) \times 5 = 4 + 7 \times 5 = 4 + 35 = 39 \neq 55$

Using Parentheses and Brackets (page 20)

41. Correct Answer: B
$4 \times [(3 + 5) \times (12 - 7)] = 4 \times [8 \times 5] = 4 \times 40 = 160$
Incorrect Answers:
A. The steps inside of the parentheses and brackets were completed, but the last step (multiplying by 4) was not completed.
C. The order of operations was not followed; the parentheses around $12 - 7$ were ignored. $3 + 5$ was correctly added first, but then the sum (8) was multiplied by 12 to get 96. The sum (8) should have been multiplied by the difference of $12 - 7$.
D. $3 + 5$ was simplified and multiplied by 4, but the rest of the problem was not completed. $(12 - 7)$ was omitted.

42. Correct Answer: D
$[(8^2 \div 4) + (3 \times 9)] - 6 = [(64 \div 4) + (3 \times 9)] - 6 = [16 + 27] - 6 = 43 - 6 = 37$
Incorrect Answers:
A. 8^2 was simplified to 16 (8×2) instead of 64 (8×8).
B. 6 was not subtracted.
C. 8^2 was simplified to 8 instead of 64 (8×8).

43. Correct Answer: C
$[7 \times (45 \div 9)] + 236 = [7 \times 5] + 236 = 35 + 236 = 271$
Incorrect Answers:
A. The order of operations was not followed. In step two, 236 was added to 5 (from $45 \div 9$), and then the sum was multiplied by 7; 236 should have been added to the product of 7×5.
B. In step 3, 35 and 236 were multiplied instead of added.
D. The steps inside the parentheses and brackets were completed, but 236 was not added at the end.

44. Correct Answer: D
Replace *n* with 2: $2 \times [(2.3 \times 7.1) - (4.21 + 9.8)] = 2 \times [16.33 - 14.01] = 2 \times 2.32 = 4.64$
Incorrect Answers:
A. The final step was not completed; 2 was not substituted for *n*.
B. The order of operations was not followed; the problem was completed from left to right.
C. The order of operations was not followed. In step two, 2 was multiplied by 16.33 instead of by the difference of 16.33 and 14.01.

Finding Common Denominators (page 21)

45. Correct Answer: D
List the multiples of the denominators (5 and 4), then use the *least common* multiple as the common denominator (20). Rename both fractions using 20 as the common denominator. Multiply the numerator and the denominator of $\frac{2}{5}$ by 4 to get $\frac{8}{20}$, and multiply the numerator and the denominator of $\frac{3}{4}$ by 5 to get $\frac{15}{20}$.
Incorrect Answers:
A. The correct common denominator was used, but the numerators of the fractions were replaced by the factors used to get the common denominator of each of the fractions.
B. The correct common denominator was used, but the numerators were not renamed.
C. $\frac{2}{5}$ remained the same, and the denominator of $\frac{3}{4}$ was unjustifiably changed to 5 while the numerator remained the same.

46. Correct Answer: C

List the multiples of the denominators (5 and 3), then use the *least common* multiple as the common denominator (15). Rename both fractions using 15 as the common denominator. Multiply the numerator and the denominator of $\frac{3}{5}$ by 3 to get $\frac{9}{15}$, and multiply the numerator and the denominator of $\frac{2}{3}$ by 5 to get $\frac{10}{15}$.

Incorrect Answers:

A. The correct common denominator was used, but the numerator of $\frac{2}{3}$ was not renamed.

B. The correct common denominator was used, but the numerators of the fractions were replaced by the factors used to get the common denominator of each of the fractions.

D. The denominator of $\frac{2}{3}$ was unjustifiably changed to 5 while the numerator remained the same; $\frac{2}{5}$ is not equivalent to $\frac{2}{3}$.

47. Correct Answer: C

List the multiples of the denominators (4 and 3). 12 is the *least common* multiple of 4 and 3.

Incorrect Answers:

A. 7 is not a multiple of 4 or 3.

B. 8 is not a multiple of 3.

D. 6 is not a multiple of 4.

48. Correct Answer: B

List the multiples of the denominators (6 and 4), then use the *least common* multiple (12) as the common denominator. Rename both fractions using 12 as the common denominator. Multiply the numerator and the denominator of $\frac{5}{6}$ by 2 to get $\frac{10}{12}$, and multiply the numerator and the denominator of $\frac{3}{4}$ by 3 to get $\frac{9}{12}$.

Incorrect Answers:

A. The correct common denominator was used, but the numerators were not renamed.

C. The correct common denominator was used, but the numerators of the fractions were replaced by the factors used to get the common denominator of each of the fractions.

D. The numerator of $\frac{3}{4}$ was not renamed.

Adding and Subtracting Fractions with Unlike Denominators *(page 22)*

49. Correct Answer: B

Find the least common denominator of the two fractions (30). Rename both fractions using the common denominator. Multiply the numerator and denominator of $\frac{1}{5}$ by 6 to get $\frac{6}{30}$, and multiply the numerator and denominator of $\frac{3}{6}$ by 5 to get $\frac{15}{30}$. Add the numerators, write the sum over the common denominator, and simplify: $\frac{21}{30} = \frac{7}{10}$.

Incorrect Answers:

A. The wrong operation (subtraction) was used.

C. The answer was not simplified.

D. The numerators were added incorrectly.

50. Correct Answer: A

Add the amount of yellow paint ($\frac{2}{3}$ cup) to the amount of blue paint ($\frac{1}{4}$ cup) Samantha mixed together. First, create equivalent fractions with a common denominator: $\frac{2}{3} = \frac{8}{12}$ and $\frac{1}{4} = \frac{3}{12}$. Then, add the numerators together.

Incorrect Answers:

B. An error occurred when converting $\frac{1}{4}$ to an equivalent fraction; $\frac{4}{12}$ was used instead of $\frac{3}{12}$.

C. The wrong operation (subtraction) was used.

D. An error occurred when converting $\frac{2}{3}$ to an equivalent fraction; $\frac{6}{12}$ was used instead of $\frac{8}{12}$, then the sum ($\frac{9}{12}$) was reduced.

51. Correct Answer: D

Find the least common denominator of the two fractions (24). Rename both fractions using the common denominator. Multiply the numerator and denominator of $\frac{4}{8}$ by 3 to get $\frac{12}{24}$, and multiply the numerator and denominator of $\frac{3}{12}$ by 2 to get $\frac{6}{24}$. Subtract the numerators, write the difference over the common denominator, and simplify: $\frac{6}{24} = \frac{1}{4}$.

Incorrect Answers:

A. $\frac{12}{24}$ was the ammount of gas only.

B. The wrong operation (addition) was used.

C. The numerators and denominators were added together.

52. Correct Answer: C

Subtract the amount of punch Julia drank ($\frac{3}{12}$ gallon) from the total amount of punch she made ($\frac{3}{4}$ gallon). First, create equivalent fractions with a common denominator. The least common denominator is 12, so $\frac{3}{12}$ stays the same and $\frac{3}{4}$ becomes $\frac{9}{12}$. Then, subtract the numerators and simplify: $\frac{6}{12} = \frac{1}{2}$.

Incorrect Answers:

A. The answer was not simplified.

B. The wrong operation (addition) was used.

D. An error occurred when subtracting the numerators.

Adding and Subtracting Mixed Numbers *(page 23)*

53. Correct Answer: D

Add to find how many inches of string Luca needs in all. Find the least common denominator of the fractional part of the mixed numbers (12). Rename $\frac{1}{3}$ by multiplying the denominator and the numerator by 4: $\frac{4}{12}$. Add the fractional parts of the mixed numbers: $\frac{4}{12} + \frac{4}{12} = \frac{8}{12}$. Simplify: $\frac{8}{12} = \frac{2}{3}$. Then add the whole numbers: $8 + 3 = 11$.

Incorrect Answers:

A. The numerators and the denominators of the mixed numbers were added together.

B. The wrong operation (subtraction) was used.

C. The answer was not simplified.

54. Correct Answer: C

Subtract the amount of lemonade sold ($2\frac{7}{8}$ gallons) from the amount of lemonade ($4\frac{5}{8}$ gallons) the squad made. First, rename $4\frac{5}{8}$ to $3\frac{13}{8}$. Then subtract the fractions and simplify: $\frac{13}{8} - \frac{7}{8} = \frac{6}{8} = \frac{3}{4}$. Subtract the whole numbers: $3 - 2 = 1$.

Incorrect Answers:

A. $4\frac{5}{8}$ was not renamed, and the fractional parts of the subtrahend and minuend were reversed ($\frac{5}{8}$ was subtracted from $\frac{7}{8}$).

B. The answer was not simplified.

D. The wrong operation (addition) was used.

Explanations for Test A Answers *(cont.)*

55. Correct Answer: B
Subtract to find how much sand Danny has left. Find the least common denominator of the fractional part of the mixed numbers (6). Rename $\frac{1}{2}$ by multiplying the denominator and the numerator by 3: $\frac{3}{6}$. Subtract the fractional parts of the mixed numbers: $\frac{5}{6} - \frac{3}{6} = \frac{2}{6}$. Simplify: $\frac{2}{6} = \frac{1}{3}$. Then subtract the whole numbers: $5 - 4 = 1$.
Incorrect Answers:
A. The answer was not simplified.
C. The wrong operation (addition) was used to solve, and the answer was not simplified.
D. An error occurred when simplifying $1\frac{2}{6}$.

56. Correct Answer: C
Add the number of hours Nicholas surfed on Saturday to the number of hours he surfed on Sunday. Find the least common denominator of the fractional part of the mixed numbers (8). Rename $\frac{3}{4}$ by multiplying the denominator and the numerator by 2: $\frac{6}{8}$. Add the fractional parts of the mixed numbers: $\frac{6}{8} + \frac{3}{8} = \frac{9}{8}$. Simplify: $\frac{9}{8} = 1\frac{1}{8}$. Then add the whole numbers, remembering to include the 1 from $1\frac{1}{8}$: $1 + 2 + 2 = 5$.
Incorrect Answers:
A. The answer was not simplified.
B. The wrong operation (subtraction) was used.
D. No common denominator was used, and the numerators and denominators of the mixed numbers were added together.

Multiplying Fractions *(page 24)*

57. Correct Answer: D
Multiply the numerators ($2 \times 5 = 10$) and the denominators ($5 \times 8 = 40$). Simplify: $\frac{10}{40} = \frac{1}{4}$.
Incorrect Answers:
A. The answer was not simplified.
B. The wrong operation was used; the fractions were incorrectly added together.
C. The denominators were multiplied, but the numerators were added.

58. Correct Answer: B
Multiply the numerators ($4 \times 3 = 12$), multiply the denominators ($9 \times 10 = 90$), and simplify: $\frac{12}{90} = \frac{2}{15}$.
Incorrect Answers:
A. The answer was not simplified.
C. The answer was not completely simplified.
D. The wrong operation was used; the fractions were incorrectly added together.

59. Correct Answer: C
$\frac{3}{4}$ of the total money raised will be spent on the playground. $\frac{2}{3}$ of the amount allocated for the playground will be spent on equipment. Multiply and simplify: $\frac{2}{3} \times \frac{3}{4} = \frac{6}{12} = \frac{1}{2}$.
Incorrect Answers:
A. The answer was not simplified.
B. The wrong operation was used; the fractions were incorrectly added together.
D. The denominators were multiplied, but the numerators were added.

60. Correct Answer: C
Multiply the amount of pizza Angie ate ($\frac{2}{8}$ of the pizza) by the amount of pizza Chrissie ate ($\frac{1}{2}$ as much) to find out how much pizza Chrissie ate ($\frac{1}{8}$ of the pizza).
Incorrect Answers:
A. The answer was not simplified.
B. The wrong operation was used; the fractions were incorrectly added.
D. The wrong operation (addition) was used.

Multiplying Fractions and Whole Numbers
(page 25)

61. Correct Answer: A
Write the whole number as an improper fraction ($\frac{25}{1}$). Multiply the numerators (3×25), multiply the denominators (4×1), and simplify: $\frac{75}{4} = 18\frac{3}{4}$.
Incorrect Answers:
B. The answer was not simplified.
C. The wrong operation was used; the fractions were incorrectly added.
D. $\frac{3}{4}$ was multiplied by $\frac{1}{25}$ instead of by $\frac{25}{1}$.

62. Correct Answer: D
Multiply the number of boxes ($\frac{1}{2}$) of candy bars Helen sold by 3 to find out how many boxes of candy bars Sandy sold: $\frac{1}{2} \times \frac{3}{1} = \frac{3}{2} = 1\frac{1}{2}$.
Incorrect Answers:
A. $\frac{1}{2}$ was multiplied by $\frac{1}{3}$ instead of by $\frac{3}{1}$.
B. The answer was not simplified.
C. The wrong operation (addition) was used.

63. Correct Answer: C
Write the whole number as an improper fraction ($\frac{35}{1}$). Multiply the numerators (35×2), multiply the denominators (1×7), and simplify: $\frac{70}{7} = 10$.
Incorrect Answers:
A. The answer was not simplified.
B. $\frac{2}{7}$ was multiplied by $\frac{1}{35}$ instead of by $\frac{35}{1}$.
D. The fractions were cross-multiplied (35×7 and 1×2).

64. Correct Answer: D
Richard grows grapes on $\frac{3}{4}$ of his 9 acres. *Of* means multiply: $\frac{3}{4} \times 9 = \frac{27}{4} = 6\frac{3}{4}$.
Incorrect Answers:
A. The wrong operation (addition) was used.
B. $\frac{3}{4}$ was multiplied by $\frac{1}{9}$ instead of by $\frac{9}{1}$.
C. The answer was not simplified.

Dividing Fractions and Whole Numbers *(page 26)*

65. Correct Answer: C
Convert the whole number 9 to an improper fraction ($\frac{9}{1}$), change the division to multiplication, and change the divisor to its reciprocal ($\frac{7}{3}$): $\frac{9}{1} \times \frac{7}{3} = \frac{63}{3} = 21$.
Incorrect Answers:
A. Division was changed to multiplication, but the reciprocal of $\frac{3}{7}$ ($\frac{7}{3}$) was not used.
B. The dividend ($\frac{9}{1}$) was replaced with its reciprocal instead of replacing the divisor ($\frac{3}{7}$) with its reciprocal.
D. The numerators were divided ($9 \div 3$) and written over the existing denominator.

Explanations for Test A Answers *(cont.)*

66. Correct Answer: D

Divide the amount of lemonade ($\frac{1}{2}$ gallon) by the amount of iced tea (4 gallons) to find out how much lemonade will be added to each gallon of the iced tea. To divide, change the divisor to its reciprocal and multiply: $\frac{1}{2} \div 4 = \frac{1}{2} \times \frac{1}{4} = \frac{1}{8}$.

Incorrect Answers:

A. The divisor and the dividend were reversed: $4 \div \frac{1}{2}$ instead of $\frac{1}{2} \div 4$.

B. $\frac{4}{1}$ was not changed to its reciprocal before multiplying.

C. Both $\frac{4}{1}$ and $\frac{1}{2}$ were changed to their reciprocals before multiplying.

67. Correct Answer: B

Convert the whole number 5 to an improper fraction ($\frac{5}{1}$), change the division to multiplication, and change the divisor to its reciprocal ($\frac{1}{5}$): $\frac{5}{8} \times \frac{1}{5} = \frac{5}{40} = \frac{1}{8}$.

Incorrect Answers:

A. An error occured when reducing $\frac{5}{40}$.

C. $\frac{5}{1}$ was not changed to its reciprocal before multiplying.

D. The answer was not simplified.

68. Correct Answer: D

Divide the amount of salt ($\frac{3}{4}$ ounces) by the number of ears of corn (6) to find out how much salt Kris will put on each ear of corn. To divide, change the divisor to its reciprocal and multiply: $\frac{3}{4} \div 6 = \frac{3}{4} \times \frac{1}{6} = \frac{3}{24} = \frac{1}{8}$.

Incorrect Answers:

A. The divisor and the dividend were reversed: $6 \div \frac{3}{4}$ instead of $\frac{3}{4} \div 6$.

B. $\frac{6}{1}$ was not changed to its reciprocal before multiplying.

C. The divisor and the dividend were reversed, the numerators of the fractions were divided, written over the existing denominator to get $\frac{2}{4}$, and reduced.

Multiplying and Dividing Fractions to Solve Word Problems *(page 27)*

69. Correct Answer: B

Divide the weight of the roast ($\frac{3}{4}$ lb.) by number of steaks (3) to find the weight of each steak. To divide, change the divisor to its reciprocal and multiply: $\frac{3}{4} \div 3 = \frac{3}{4} \times \frac{1}{3} = \frac{3}{12} = \frac{1}{4}$.

Incorrect Answers:

A. The answer was not simplified.

C. The divisor and the dividend were reversed: $3 \div \frac{3}{4}$ instead of $\frac{3}{4} \div 3$.

D. 3 was not changed to its reciprocal before multiplying.

70. Correct Answer: C

Divide the amount of juice ($\frac{1}{2}$ bottle) by the number of nieces (4) Wanda will evenly divide the juice between to find out how much juice each of the nieces will have with breakfast. To divide, change the divisor to its reciprocal and multiply: $\frac{1}{2} \div 4 = \frac{1}{2} \times \frac{1}{4} = \frac{1}{8}$.

Incorrect Answers:

A. 4 was not changed to its reciprocal before multiplying.

B. The divisor and the dividend were reversed: $4 \div \frac{1}{2}$ instead of $\frac{1}{2} \div 4$.

D. Both $\frac{1}{2}$ and $\frac{4}{1}$ were changed to their reciprocals before multiplying.

71. Correct Answer: B

Multiply the amount of aluminum cans Steve collected ($\frac{4}{5}$ of a barrel) by how many more Todd collected (5 times more) to find out how many barrels of aluminum cans Todd collected: $\frac{4}{5} \times \frac{5}{1} = \frac{20}{5} = 4$.

Incorrect Answers:

A. $\frac{4}{5}$ was multiplied by $\frac{1}{5}$ instead of by $\frac{5}{1}$.

C. The answer was not simplified.

D. $\frac{20}{5}$ was incorrectly reduced.

72. Correct Answer: D

They spent $\frac{1}{4}$ *of* their 5 hours at the lake on paddleboats. *Of* means multiply: $\frac{1}{4} \times \frac{5}{1} = \frac{5}{4} = 1\frac{1}{4}$.

Incorrect Answers:

A. The wrong operation (addition) was used.

B. $\frac{1}{4}$ was multiplied by $\frac{1}{5}$ instead of by $\frac{5}{1}$.

C. The answer was not simplified.

Converting Measurement Units *(page 28)*

73. Correct Answer: C

36 in. = 1 yd., so 36 in. × 9 yd. = 324 in.

Incorrect Answers:

A. 108 in. equals 9 ft., not 9 yd.

B. 24 ft. = 8 yd.

D. 27 ft. and 9 in. = 9 yd. and 9 in.

74. Correct Answer: B

1 g = 1,000 mg, so 5,000 g × 1,000 mg per g = 5,000,000 mg.

Incorrect Answers:

A. 1,000 g = 1 kg, so 5,000 g ÷ 1,000 g per kg = 5 kg, not 50 kg.

C. 1 g = 1,000 mg, 5,000 g × 1,000 mg per g = 5,000,000 mg, not 50,000 mg.

D. 1,000 g = 1 kg, so 1,000 g per kilogram × 500 kg = 500,000 g, not 5,000 g.

75. Correct Answer: D

1,000 mL = 1 L. 500 mL × 12 players = 6,000 mL. 6,000 mL ÷ 1,000 mL per L = 6 L.

Incorrect Answers:

A. 41 $\frac{2}{3}$ mL was calculated by incorrectly dividing 500 mL by 12 players instead of multiplying.

B. 5 L = 5,000 mL, but Brandon needs 6,000 mL or 6 L of juice.

C. 5 L and 500 mL = 5,500 mL, but Brandon needs 6,000 mL or 6 L of juice.

76. Correct Answer: A

1 lb. = 16 oz., so 64 lb. × 16 oz. per lb. = 1,024 oz., and $\frac{1}{2}$ lb. = 8 oz. 1,024 oz. + 8 oz. = 1,032 oz.

Incorrect Answers:

B. 1,024 oz. = 64 lb.; it does not include the $\frac{1}{2}$ lb.

C. 774 oz. would equal 12 oz. per lb., not 16 oz. per lb.

D. *About 4 oz.* was calculated by dividing 64 lb. by 16 oz. instead of multiplying.

Ordered Pairs *(page 29)*

77. Correct Answer: C

Move right 2 and up 4; there is a circle.

Incorrect Answers:

A. The triangle is located at (5,3).

B. The square is located at (4,2).

D. The star is located at (7,1).

Explanations for Test A Answers *(cont.)*

78. Correct Answer: A
Move right 5 and up 3; there is a triangle.
Incorrect Answers:
B. The square is located at (4,2).
C. The circle is located at (2,4).
D. The star is located at (7,1).

79. Correct Answer: D
Point *B* is located 6 units to the right and 3 units above the origin: (6,3).
Incorrect Answers:
A. Point *E* is located at (3,6).
B. Point *C* is located at (2,8).
C. Point *F* is located at (0,2).

80. Correct Answer: B
Point *D* is located 4 units to the right and 0 units above the origin: (4,0).
Incorrect Answers:
A. Point *C* is located at (2,8).
C. Point *F* is located at (0,2).
D. Point *A* is located at (9,1).

Line Plots *(page 30)*

81. Correct Answer: D
greatest = $8\frac{1}{2}$ pounds; least = $3\frac{1}{2}$ pounds
Incorrect Answers:
A. $8\frac{1}{2}$ pounds > $7\frac{1}{2}$ pounds; $3\frac{1}{2}$ pounds < $5\frac{1}{2}$ pounds
B. $8\frac{1}{2}$ pounds > $7\frac{1}{2}$ pounds; $3\frac{1}{2}$ pounds < $4\frac{1}{2}$ pounds.
C. $8\frac{1}{2}$ is the greatest number of pounds, but $3\frac{1}{2}$ pounds < 5 pounds.

82. Correct Answer: B
$6\frac{1}{2}$ occurs 4 times in the data, and $8\frac{1}{2}$ occurs 2 times: 4–2 = 2.
Incorrect Answers:
A. A counting or subtraction error occurred.
C. A counting or subtraction error occurred.
D. The wrong operation (addition) was used.

83. Correct Answer: C
There are 20 data values listed, so 20 Boy Scouts sold candy.
Incorrect Answers:
A. B. D. These responses do not match the dats.

84. Correct Answer: A
$4\frac{1}{2}$ occurs 4 times in the data, so there would be 4 Xs above $4\frac{1}{2}$ pounds on the line plot.
Incorrect Answers:
B. C. D. These responses do not match the data.

Volume of Solid Figures *(page 31)*

85. Correct Answer: B
2 rows × 4 cubes in each row = 8 cubic units
Incorrect Answers:
A. 12 cubic units was calculated by counting the faces on the top and the front of the object.
C. 4 cubic units was calculated by counting one row of the object.
D. 14 cubic units was calculated by counting all the visible faces of the cubes.

86. Correct Answer: D
The bottom layer has 4 cubes and the top layer has 2 cubes: 4 + 2 = 6 cubic units.
Incorrect Answers:
A. 4 cubic units was calculated by counting only the cubes whose tops are visible; two cubes are under the top layer.
B. 12 cubic units was calculated by counting all the visible faces of the cubes.
C. 8 cubic units was calculated by counting the faces on the top and the front of the object.

87. Correct Answer: A
18 cubes in each layer × 2 layers = 36 cubic units
Incorrect Answers:
B. 18 cubic units includes only 1 layer of cubes instead of 2 layers.
C. 40 cubic units was calculated by counting all the visible faces of the cubes.
D. 54 cubic units includes 3 layers of cubes instead of 2 layers.

88. Correct Answer: C
12 cubes in each layer × 2 layers = 24 cubic units
Incorrect Answers:
A. 12 cubic units is the number of cubic units in one layer.
B. *Units* is an incorrect label.
D. 14 cubic units was calculated by adding the 12 cubes in one layer and the 2 from the 2 layers.

Volume of Regular and Irregular Rectangular Prisms *(page 32)*

89. Correct Answer: C
$V = l \times w \times h$: 6 ft. × 2 ft. × 5 ft. = 60 ft.^{3}
Incorrect Answers:
A. Ft.^{2} is the label for area, not volume.
B. 12 ft.^{3} was calculated by multiplying $l \times w$; h was not included.
D. 13 ft.^{3} was calculated by adding $l + w + h$ instead of multiplying.

90. Correct Answer: B
$V = l \times w \times h$: 7 cm × 4 cm × 3 cm = 84 cm^3
Incorrect Answers:
A. 14 cm^3 was calculated by adding $l + w + h$ instead of multiplying.
C. 28 cm^3 was calculated by multiplying $l \times w$; h was not included.
D. 12 cm^3 was calculated by multiplying $w \times h$; l was not included.

91. Correct Answer: D
$V = l \times w \times h$
Volume of Rectangular Prism 1 = 4 m × 3 m × 7 m = 84 m^3;
Volume of Rectangular Prism 2 = 2 m × 1 m × 3 m = 6 m^3;
Total Volume = 84 m^3 + 6 m^3 = 90 m^3
Incorrect Answers:
A. 84 m^3 is the volume of rectangular prism 1; it does not include the entire figure.
B. 504 m^3 was calculated by multiplying the lengths, widths, and heights of both prisms together:
4 × 3 × 7 × 2 × 1 × 3 = 504 m^3.
C. The volume of rectangular prism 2 was calculated using 7 m as the height instead of 3 m.

92. Correct Answer: C

$V = l \times w \times h$

Volume of Rectangular Prism 1 = 4 in. × 2 in. × 3 in. = 24 in.^{3}
Volume of Rectangular Prism 2 = 4 in. × 3 in. × 6 in. = 72 in.^{3}
Total Volume = 24 in.^{3} + 72 in.^{3} = 96 in.^{3}

Incorrect Answers:

A. In.^{2} is the label for area, not volume.
B. 72 in.^{3} is the volume of rectangular Prism 2; it does not include the entire figure.
D. 24 in.^{3} is the volume of rectangular Prism 1; it does not include the entire figure.

Area of Rectangles with Fractional Sides

(page 33)

93. Correct Answer: A

$A = l \times w$

Convert the mixed numbers to improper fractions:
$2\frac{5}{10} = \frac{25}{10}$ and $1\frac{3}{5} = \frac{8}{5}$.
Cross cancel the numerator 25 with the denominator 5 and the numerator 8 with the denominator 10 to get $\frac{5}{5} \times \frac{4}{1} = \frac{20}{5} = 4$.

Incorrect Answers:

B. The answer was not simplified completely.
C. An error occurred when multiplying or when reducing the product.
D. The mixed numbers were not renamed as improper fractions before multiplying.

94. Correct Answer: C

$A = l \times w$

Convert the whole number 4 to an improper fraction, and convert the mixed number $3\frac{1}{2}$ to an improper fraction:
$\frac{4}{1} \times \frac{7}{2} = \frac{28}{2} = 14$.

Incorrect Answers:

A. The whole number and the mixed number $3\frac{1}{2}$ were not renamed as improper fractions before multiplying; the whole numbers were multiplied, and then the fractions were added.
B. The answer was not simplified.
D. $3\frac{1}{2}$ was multiplied by $\frac{1}{4}$ instead of by $\frac{4}{1}$.

95. Correct Answer: D

$A = l \times w$

Rewrite the mixed numbers as improper fractions:
$2\frac{1}{2} = \frac{5}{2}$ and $1\frac{3}{4} = \frac{7}{4}$. $\frac{5}{2} \times \frac{7}{4} = \frac{35}{8} = 4\frac{3}{8}$.

Incorrect Answers:

A. The mixed numbers were not renamed as improper fractions before multiplying; the whole numbers were multiplied, and then the fractions were multiplied.
B. The answer was not simplified.
C. The length and width were added instead of multiplied.

96. Correct Answer: B

$A = l \times w$

Rewrite the mixed numbers as improper fractions to get $\frac{25}{2} \times \frac{61}{5}$.
Cross cancel the numerator 25 with the denominator 5 to get
$\frac{5}{2} \times \frac{61}{1} = \frac{305}{2} = 152\frac{1}{2}$.

Incorrect Answers:

A. The mixed numbers were not renamed as improper fractions before multiplying; the whole numbers were multiplied, and then the fractions were multiplied.
C. The length and width were added instead of multiplied.
D. The answer was not simplified.

Classifying Two-dimensional Shapes *(page 34)*

97. Correct Answer: B

The figure has four sides which indicates it is a quadrilateral, and it has one pair of parallel sides which indicates it is a trapezoid.

Incorrect Answers:

A. A rectangle has two pairs of parallel sides and four right angles; a parallelogram has two pairs of parallel sides.
C. A parallelogram has two pairs of parallel sides.
D. A parallelogram has two pairs of parallel sides; a square has four right angles and four sides with equal length.

98. Correct Answer: B

The figure has four sides which indicates it is a quadrilateral, opposite sides are parallel which indicates it is a parallelogram, and all four sides have equal length which indicates it is a rhombus.

Incorrect Answers:

A. It is a quadrilateral and a parallelogram, but a square is a parallelogram with four right angles.
C. It is a quadrilateral and a parallelogram, but a rectangle is a parallelogram with four right angles.
D. It is a quadrilateral and a parallelogram, but a trapezoid has exactly one pair of parallel sides.

99. Correct Answer: D

A square is a parallelogram with four right angles and four sides with equal length.

Incorrect Answers:

A. A rectangle is a parallelogram with four right angles, but not four equal sides.
B. A trapezoid is not a parallelogram and it does not have four right angles.
C. A rhombus is a parallelogram with four sides of equal length, but it does not have four right angles.

100. Correct Answer: C

A square is also a rhombus because it is a parallelogram with four sides of equal length.

Incorrect Answers:

A. A rectangle does not have four sides of equal length.
B. A trapezoid is not a parallelogram and does not have four sides of equal length.
D. The correct answer is *square*, so *none of the above* is incorrect.

Explanations for Test B Answers

Multiplying Multi-digit Numbers *(page 35)*

1. Correct Answer: B

Multiply the monthly payment by the number of payments to find out how much Nicholas will pay for the bike:
$85 × 14 = $1,190.

Incorrect Answers:

A. The two tens regrouped from multiplying 4 × 5 were not included in the partial product.

C. The 1 in the tens place of 14 was multiplied as 1 one instead of as 1 ten.

D. An error occurred in the hundreds column when adding the partial products.

2. Correct Answer: D

Follow steps 1–6.

1. Write 19 under 49.
2. Multiply 49 by 9 ones to get 441 (remember to regroup).
3. Write the partial product (441).
4. Multiply 49 by 1 ten to get 49 tens.
5. Write the partial product (490).
6. Add the partial products: 441 + 490 = 931.

Incorrect Answers:

A. An error occurred in the tens column when adding the partial products.

B. A regrouping error occurred in the hundreds column when adding the partial products.

C. The 1 in 19 was multiplied as 1 one instead of as 1 ten.

3. Correct Answer: C

Follow steps 1–6.

1. Write 23 under 726.
2. Multiply 726 by 3 ones to get 2,178 (remember to regroup).
3. Write the partial product (2,178).
4. Multiply 726 by 2 tens to get 1,452 tens (remember to regroup).
5. Write the partial product (14,520).
6. Add the partial products: 2,178 + 14,520 = 16,698.

Incorrect Answers:

A. The 2 in 23 was multiplied as 2 ones instead of as 2 tens.

B. When multiplying the 2 in the tens place by 7 in the hundreds place, the result was recorded as 21 instead of 14.

D. An error occurred in the hundreds place when adding the partial products.

4. Correct Answer: A

Multiply the number of miles the family drove each day by the number of days they drove to find the total number of miles they drove on the road trip: 175 miles per day × 12 days = 2,100 miles.

Incorrect Answers:

B. The 1 in 12 was multiplied as 1 one instead of as 1 ten.

C. A regrouping error occurred in the hundreds column when adding the partial products.

D. A regrouping error occurred in the thousands column when adding the partial products.

Dividing by Two-digit Divisors *(page 36)*

5. Correct Answer: D

Divide the total number of juice boxes needed by the number of juice boxes in each carton to find the number of cartons that should be ordered: 492 ÷ 12 = 41.

Incorrect Answers:

A. A division error occurred when dividing in step one: 49 ÷ 12 ≠ 3 because 3 × 12 = 36, leaving room for 12 to go into 49 one more time.

B. A division error occurred when dividing in step three: 12 ÷ 12 ≠ 2 because 2 × 12 = 24 and 24 is greater than 12.

C. The remainder, 0, was written instead of the quotient of 12 ÷ 12 in the last step of division.

6. Correct Answer: C

The first digit of the dividend (9) is *less* than the divisor (11), so divide 11 into the first two digits of the divisor.
DIVIDE: 96 ÷ 11 = 8. Write 8 in the quotient above 6.
MULTIPLY: 8 × 11 = 88. *SUBTRACT:* 96 − 88 = 8.
BRING DOWN: the 8 from the ones column of the dividend to form 88.
DIVIDE: 88 ÷ 11 = 8. Write 8 in the quotient above 8.
MULTIPLY: 8 × 11 = 88. *SUBTRACT:* 88 − 88 = 0.
There is nothing left to bring down; the quotient is 88.

Incorrect Answers:

A. An error occurred when dividing 96 by 11 in the first step; 11 does not go into 96 nine times.

B. An error occurred when dividing 96 by 11 in the first step; 11 goes into 96 more than seven times.

D. An error occurred when recording the answer to 88 ÷ 11 in the last step of division; the remainder is 0, not the quotient.

7. Correct Answer: B

Divide the number of students (45) by the number of students each bus can seat (12) to get 3 R9. The 3 in the quotient indicates that 3 buses will be full, and the remainder (9) indicates that an additional bus will be needed for the 9 remaining students:
1 full bus + 1 partially full bus = 4 buses.

Incorrect Answers:

A. 12 does not go into 45 five times; 12 × 5 = 60, which is greater than 45.

C. 3 buses will seat only 36 students; the remaining 9 students also need a bus.

D. The correct answer is 4 buses (*B*).

8. Correct Answer: B

The first digit of the dividend (6) is *less* than the divisor (40), so divide 40 into the first two digits of the divisor (62).
DIVIDE: 62 ÷ 40 = 1. Write 1 in the quotient above 2.
MULTIPLY: 1 × 40 = 40.
SUBTRACT: 62 − 40 = 22. *BRING DOWN:* the 4 from 624.
DIVIDE: 224 ÷ 40 = 5. Write 5 in the quotient above 4.
MULTIPLY: 5 × 40 = 200.
SUBTRACT: 224 − 200 = 24. There is nothing left to bring down, so the quotient is 15 R24.

Incorrect Answers:

A. An error occurred when subtracting in step 7: 224 − 200 ≠ 4.

C. An error occurred when dividing 224 ÷ 40 in step 5; 40 does not go into 224 six times.

D. Errors occurred when dividing in step 5 (224 ÷ 40 ≠ 6) and then when multiplying in step 6 (6 × 40 ≠ 224).

Explanations for Test B Answers *(cont.)*

Reading and Writing Decimals to Thousandths
(page 37)

9. Correct Answer: B
$70{,}000 + 1{,}000 + 600 + 50 + 4 + \frac{2}{10} + \frac{3}{100} = 71{,}654.23$
Incorrect Answers:
A. Instead of $\frac{2}{10} + \frac{3}{100}$, this is $\frac{2}{100} + \frac{3}{1{,}000}$.
C. This is $7{,}000 + 100 + 60 + 5 + \frac{4}{10} + \frac{2}{100} + \frac{3}{1{,}000}$.
D. Instead of $\frac{2}{10} + \frac{3}{100}$, this is $\frac{3}{10} + \frac{2}{100}$.

10. Correct Answer: A
$4{,}953.617 = 4{,}000 + 900 + 50 + 3 + \frac{6}{10} + \frac{1}{100} + \frac{7}{1{,}000}$
Incorrect Answers:
B. This is 40,953.617.
C. This is 4,956.17.
D. This is 5,430.617.

11. Correct Answer: C
And indicates where the decimal point belongs. *Thirty-six thousandths* indicates that the numbers after the decimal point should end in the thousandths place.
Incorrect Answers:
A. This is five and thirty-six hundredths.
B. This is five hundred thirty-six thousandths.
D. This is five and thirty-six ten thousandths.

12. Correct Answer: C
5,375.281 = five thousand three hundred seventy-five and two hundred eighty-one thousandths
Incorrect Answers:
A. *Two hundred eighty-one hundredths* = 2.81, so 5,375 + 2.81 = 5,377.81.
B. This is 53,075.281.
D. This is 5,375 + 281 = 5,656.

Interpreting Place Value *(page 38)*

13. Correct Answer: C
$1\frac{83}{1{,}000}$ = one and eighty-three thousandths = 1.083
Incorrect Answers:
A. $1.83 = 1\frac{83}{100}$
B. $0.183 = \frac{183}{1{,}000}$
D. $1.0083 = 1\frac{83}{10{,}000}$

14. Correct Answer: B
$7.75 = 7\frac{75}{100} = 7\frac{3}{4}$
Incorrect Answers:
A. 7 is a whole number; it is not part of the fraction. 75 should be the numerator of the fraction, not the denominator.
C. $\frac{775}{1{,}000} = 0.775$, not 7.75.
D. $7\frac{1}{4} = 7.25$, not 7.75.

15. Correct Answer: B
In 535,870 the 7 is worth seven tens or 70. In 537,805 the 7 is worth seven thousands or 7,000. $70 \times 100 = 7{,}000$, so 70 is 100 times less than 7,000.
Incorrect Answers:
A. The value of the number 10 times less than 7,000 is 700, not 70.
C. The value of the number 1,000 times less than 7,000 is 7, not 70.
D. The 7 in 535,870 is two *places* to the right of the 7 in 537,805, but each place value is worth *10 times less* than the place value to its left.

16. Correct Answer: C
Ten times less $= \frac{1}{10}$.
$\frac{1}{10}$ of $0.008 = \frac{1}{10} \times 0.008 = 0.1 \times 0.008 = 0.0008$
Incorrect Answers:
A. In .08, the value of the 8 is ten times *greater* than it is in 0.008.
B. In 0.008, the value of the 8 is the same as it is in 0.008.
D. In 0.8, the value of the 8 is one hundred times greater than it is in 0.008.

Comparing Decimals to Thousandths *(page 39)*

17. Correct Answer: A
8.366 comes between 8.36 and 8.37: 8.36<u>0</u>, 8.3<u>66</u>, 8.3<u>70</u>.
Incorrect Answers:
B. 8.360 = 8.36, so it does not come between 8.36 and 8.37.
C. 8.371 comes after 8.37.
D. 8.38 comes after 8.37.

18. Correct Answer: C
Ignore the decimal points to compare:
$0.\underline{6}31 > 0.\underline{6}13 > 0.\underline{6}03 > 0.\underline{6}00$.
Incorrect Answers:
A. The correct order is 5.9, 5.88, 5.878, 5.788.
B. The correct order is 9.999, 9.908, 9.822, 0.999.
D. 2.3, 2.31, 2.33, 2.39 are in order from least to greatest, not greatest to least.

19. Correct Answer: D
$1.1\underline{0}1 < 1.1\underline{1}$
Incorrect Answers:
A. $1.\underline{1}01 > 1.\underline{0}11$, not <.
B. 1.101 = 1.101, not <.
C. $1.\underline{1}01 > 1.\underline{0}1$, not <.

20. Correct Answer: B
6.6 = 6.600 is true.
Incorrect Answers:
A. $3.5\underline{3} < 3.5\underline{4}$, not >.
C. $5.\underline{8} > 5.\underline{7}6$, not <.
D. $9.\underline{0}5 < 9.\underline{5}0$, not =.

Rounding Decimals *(page 40)*

21. Correct Answer: A
To round to the nearest hundredth, look at the digit to the right of the hundredths place. Since the digit is 5, round the hundredths digit up.
Incorrect Answers:
B. 7.785 was rounded down; it should have been rounded up.
C. 7.785 was rounded to the nearest tenth.
D. 7.785 was rounded to the nearest one.

22. Correct Answer: D
To round to the nearest ten cents, look at the digit to the right of the tenths place. Since the digit is 5, round the tenths digit up.
Incorrect Answers:
A. $11.25 was rounded down; it should have been rounded up.
B. $11.25 was rounded to the nearest one dollar.
C. $11.25 was rounded to the nearest ten dollars.

23. Correct Answer: B
To round to the nearest thousandth, look at the digit to the right of the thousandths place. Since the digit (4) is less than 5, round down by leaving the digit in the thousandths place (4) the same.
Incorrect Answers:
A. 312.5344 was rounded to the nearest one.
C. 312.5344 was rounded to the nearest hundredth.
D. 312.5344 was rounded to the nearest tenth.

Explanations for Test B Answers *(cont.)*

24. Correct Answer: B
To round to the nearest hundredth, look at the digit to the right of the hundredths place. Since the digit (9) is greater than 5, round up: 68.779 ≈ 68.78.
Incorrect Answers:
A. 68.789 ≈ 68.79, not 68.78.
C. 68.773 ≈ 68.77, not 68.78.
D. 68.787 ≈ 68.79, 68.78.

Adding and Subtracting Decimals *(page 41)*

25. Correct Answer: A
Align the decimal points and write a *0* after 9.6 to subtract:

9.6*0*
– 5.73
3.87

Incorrect Answers:
B. The decimal is in the wrong place.
C. The decimal points were not aligned before subtracting; instead, the numbers were aligned flush right.
D. When subtracting the ones and tenths columns the numbers were not regrouped properly.

26. Correct Answer: C
Align the decimal points to add:

52.1
+ 65.37
117.47

Incorrect Answers:
A. The decimal points were not aligned before adding; the numbers were aligned flush right.
B. The decimal is in the wrong place.
D. The decimal is in the wrong place.

27. Correct Answer: B
32.5 L
– 27.34 L
5.16 L
Incorrect Answers:
A. The decimal is in the wrong place.
C. The wrong operation (addition) was used.
D. A *0* was not written after the 5 in 32.5, so instead of subtracting 10 – 4 in the hundredths column the 4 was just brought down.

28. Correct Answer: D
Align the decimal points to add:

43.99 in.
+ 42.7 in.
86.69 in.

Incorrect Answers:
A. The decimal points were not aligned before adding.
B. The numbers were subtracted instead of added.
C. The decimal is in the wrong place.

Multiplying and Dividing Decimals *(page 42)*

29. Correct Answer: A
16.84 ÷ 0.4 = 42.1
Incorrect Answers:
B. The decimal is in the wrong place.
C. The decimal is in the wrong place.
D. Instead of dividing 16 ÷ 4 in step one, *6* ÷ 4 was calculated. The 1 in 16.84 was ignored.

30. Correct Answer: B
8.53 × 6.3 = 53.739
Incorrect Answers:
A. The decimal is in the wrong place.
C. When multiplying 8.53 by the 6 in 6.3 a *0* place holder was not used in the partial product; the partial product was 5,118 instead of 51,180.
D. The decimal is in the wrong place.

31. Correct Answer: D
1.5 miles × 7 days = 10.5 miles
Incorrect Answers:
A. *Days* is the wrong label.
B. The wrong operation (addition) was used.
C. The decimal is in the wrong place.

32. Correct Answer: C
24.06 ÷ 0.3 = 80.2; Jake is correct.
Incorrect Answers:
A. Phillip is not correct; he put the decimal in the wrong place.
B. 8.2 is not the quotient.
D. 8.02 ≠ 80.2

Multiple-step Problems with Decimals *(page 43)*

33. Correct Answer: B
The first step is to find how much Stella paid for the puzzles in all. Multiplication is the best operation to use to find the total cost of 13 puzzles that each cost the same amount.
Incorrect Answers:
A. The problem could be solved with addition, but multiplication is the best answer because it is more efficient.
C. Subtraction is used to find the difference, not the total.
D. Division is used to separate items into equal groups, not to find the total.

34. Correct Answer: C
$2.75 × 13 = $35.75 gives the total cost for all the puzzles.
Incorrect Answers:
A. $40.00 – $2.75 = $37.25 is the amount of change Stella would get if she purchased one puzzle.
B. $2.75 + 13 puzzles = $15.75 is not possible; unlike quantities (dollars and puzzles) cannot be added. Also, it does not give the total amount spent on puzzles.
D. $40.00 + $2.75 = $42.75 is the price of one puzzle plus the amount of money Stella gave to the clerk; it does not give the total amount spent on puzzles.

35. Correct Answer: C
The total amount Stella spent on all the puzzles must be known so that amount can be subtracted from $40.00.
Incorrect Answers:
A. *The number of puzzles Stella bought* was multiplied by the price of each puzzle in step one to find how much she spent in all.
B. *Who Stella bought the puzzles for* does not matter in the solution of the problem; it is unnecessary information.
D. *How much money Stella spent for each puzzle* was multiplied by the number of puzzles Stella bought in step one to find how much she spent in all.

36. Correct Answer: D
$40.00 paid – $35.75 owed = $4.25 change
Incorrect Answers:
A. $2.75 is the price of one puzzle.
B. $75.75 was calculated by adding the amount Stella spent for all the puzzles ($35.75) to the amount she gave the clerk ($40.00).
C. $44.25 was calculated by adding $40.00 to the amount of change Stella got back from her purchase ($4.25).

Simplifying Expressions (page 44)

37. Correct Answer: D
$(8 \times 4) - (42 \div 7) + 4^3 = 32 - 6 + 64 = 90$
Incorrect Answers:
A. 4^3 was calculated as 16, instead of 64.
B. 4^3 was calculated as $4 \times 3 = 12$, instead of $4 \times 4 \times 4 = 64$.
C. 4^3 was calculated by adding the 4 to the exponent 3 to get 7, instead of $4 \times 4 \times 4 = 64$.

38. Correct Answer: C
$55 + (y \times 6) - 9 = 55 + (3 \times 6) - 9 = 55 + 18 - 9 = 64$
Incorrect Answers:
A. The order of operations was not followed; $55 + 3$ was calculated first, $6 - 9$ was incorrectly calculated as 3, then the numbers were multiplied: $58 \times 3 = 174$.
B. The order of operations was not followed; $55 + 3$ was calculated first to get $58 \times 6 - 9 = 339$.
D. $55 + 18 = 73$: In the last step, the 9 was not subtracted.

39. Correct Answer: B
$(3 \times 7) \times (10 - 3^2) = 21 \times (10 - 9) = 21 \times 1 = 21$
Incorrect Answers:
A. 3^2 was calculated as 5 by adding the 3 to the exponent 2, instead of $3 \times 3 = 9$.
C. 3^2 was calculated as $3 \times 2 = 6$, instead of 9.
D. The order of operations was not followed; instead of completing the calculations inside of the parentheses first $(10 - 9)$ then multiplying 21×1, 21 was multiplied by 10.

40. Correct Answer: A
$72 \div 2^3 + (7 - 2) = 72 \div 8 + 5 = 9 + 5 = 14$
Incorrect Answers:
B. $(8 + 9) \times (3 - 2) + 1 = 17 \times 1 + 1 = 17 + 1 = 18$, not 17.
C. $(36 \div 6) \times (3^2 - 5) = 6 \times (9 - 5) = 6 \times 4 = 24$, not 6.
D. $(3 \times 9) - (4 + 2 + 3) = 27 - 9 = 18$, not 21.

Using Parentheses and Brackets (page 45)

41. Correct Answer: C
$11 + [(3 \times 2^3) - (4 \times 5)] \times 3 =$
$11 + [(3 \times 8) - 20] \times 3 =$
$11 + [24 - 20] \times 3 = 11 + (4 \times 3) =$
$11 + 12 = 23$
Incorrect Answers:
A. 2^3 was calculated as $2 \times 3 = 6$ instead of $2 \times 2 \times 2 = 8$, resulting in $3 \times 6 = 18$ instead of $3 \times 8 = 24$. Then $18 - 20$ was incorrectly calculated as 2.
B. The order of operations was not followed; the operations were performed from left to right, ignoring brackets and parentheses.
D. The order of operations was not followed in the last step; $11 + 4$ was added before multiplying 4×3.

42. Correct Answer: A
$360 - [(12 \times 6) \times (16 \div 8)] + 5 =$
$360 - [72 \times 2] + 5 =$
$360 - 144 + 5 = 221$
Incorrect Answers:
B. 5 was not added in the last step.
C. After simplifying the quantities in the parentheses, the order of operations was not followed, and the expression was simplified from left to right.
D. In the last step, 144 was added to 5 instead of being subtracted from 360; *360* was not included in the calculations.

43. Correct Answer: D
$[(6 \times r) - (4 + 9)] \times 7 =$
$[(6 \times 4) - (4 + 9)] \times 7 =$
$[24 - 13] \times 7 = 11 \times 7 = 77$
Incorrect Answers:
A. The order of operations was not followed; 13×7 was calculated (to get 91) before $24 - 13$. Then, the order of $24 - 91$ was reversed to get 67.
B. The order of operations was not followed; brackets and parentheses were ignored.
C. The last step was skipped; after subtracting $24 - 13$, the difference was not multiplied by 7.

44. Correct Answer: B
$52 - 8 + [(25 \div 5) \times (36 \div 4)] =$
$52 - 8 + [5 \times 9] =$
$52 - 8 + 45 = 89$
Incorrect Answers:
A. (5×9) was added instead of multiplied.
C. $(36 \div 4)$ was not included in the solution.
D. The order of operations was not followed; $52 - 8$ was subtracted to get 44, 44 was multiplied by 5 $(25 \div 5)$, and then the product was multiplied by 9 $(36 \div 4)$.

Finding Common Denominators (page 46)

45. Correct Answer: C
List the multiples of the denominators (7 and 3), then use the *least common* multiple (21) as the common denominator. Rename both fractions using 21 as the common denominator. Multiply the numerator and the denominator of $\frac{2}{7}$ by 3 to get $\frac{6}{21}$, and multiply the numerator and the denominator of $\frac{2}{3}$ by 7 to get $\frac{14}{21}$.
Incorrect Answers:
A. $\frac{2}{7}$ remained the same, and the denominator of $\frac{2}{3}$ was unjustifiably changed to 7 while the numerator remained the same.
B. The correct common denominator was used, but the numerators were not renamed.
D. The correct common denominator was used, but the numerators of the fractions were replaced by the factors used to get the common denominator of each of the fractions.

46. Correct Answer: D
List the multiples of the denominators (6 and 4), then use the *least common* multiple (12) as the common denominator. Rename both fractions using 12 as the common denominator. Multiply the numerator and the denominator of $\frac{5}{6}$ by 2 to get $\frac{10}{12}$, and multiply the numerator and the denominator of $\frac{1}{4}$ by 3 to get $\frac{3}{12}$.

Explanations for Test B Answers *(cont.)*

46. Incorrect Answers:

- **A.** The correct common denominator was used, but the numerators of the fractions were replaced by the factors used to get the common denominator of each of the fractions.
- **B.** The correct common denominator was used, but the numerators of the fractions were not renamed.
- **C.** $\frac{5}{6}$ remained the same, and the denominator of $\frac{1}{4}$ was unjustifiably changed to 6 while the numerator remained the same.

47. Correct Answer: D

List the multiples of the denominators (2 and 9), then use the *least common* multiple (18) as the common denominator. Rename both fractions using 18 as the common denominator. Multiply the numerator and the denominator of $\frac{1}{2}$ by 9 to get $\frac{9}{18}$, and multiply the numerator and the denominator of $\frac{2}{9}$ by 2 to get $\frac{4}{18}$.

Incorrect Answers:

- **A.** The correct common denominator was used, but the numerators of the fractions were replaced by the factors used to find the common denominator of each of the fractions.
- **B.** The correct common denominator was used, but the numerators were not renamed.
- **C.** $\frac{1}{2}$ remained the same, and the denominator of $\frac{2}{9}$ was unjustifiably changed to 2 while the numerator remained the same.

48. Correct Answer: B

List the multiples of the denominators (8 and 4), then use the *least common* multiple (8) as the common denominator. $\frac{3}{8}$ remains the same; multiply the numerator and the denominator of $\frac{1}{4}$ by 2 to get $\frac{2}{8}$.

Incorrect Answers:

- **A.** An incorrect common denominator was found by adding the two denominators together, and numerators remained the same.
- **C.** The denominator of $\frac{1}{4}$ was correctly changed to 8, but the numerator was not renamed.
- **D.** $\frac{1}{4}$ was incorrectly renamed: $\frac{1}{4} \neq \frac{4}{8}$.

Adding and Subtracting Fractions with Unlike Denominators *(page 47)*

49. Correct Answer: C

To find how many miles Lily walked in all, add the distances. To add, find the least common denominator of the two fractions (18), and rename both fractions using the common denominator. Rename $\frac{4}{9}$ by multiplying the denominator and the numerator by 2 to get $\frac{8}{18}$. Rename $\frac{2}{6}$ by multiplying the numerator and denominator by 3 to get $\frac{6}{18}$. Add the numerators, place the sum over the common denominator, and simplify: $\frac{8}{18} + \frac{6}{18} = \frac{14}{18} = \frac{7}{9}$.

Incorrect Answers:

- **A.** The distances were subtracted instead of added.
- **B.** The answer was not simplified.
- **D.** A common denominator was not found, the numerators and denominators of the fractions were added to get $\frac{6}{15}$, and the answer was simplified.

50. Correct Answer: C

Add the amount of yogurt to the amount of pineapple to find out how much smoothie Chrissy made: $\frac{1}{2} + \frac{1}{3} = \frac{3}{6} + \frac{2}{6} = \frac{5}{6}$ cup.

Incorrect Answers:

- **A.** The numerators were added together and the denominators were added together.
- **B.** The wrong operation (subtraction) was used.
- **D.** The answer was not simplified.

51. Correct Answer: D

Subtract to find how much ribbon will be left. Find the least common denominator of the two fractions (24), and rename both fractions using the common denominator.

Multiply the numerator and denominator of $\frac{7}{8}$ by 3 to get $\frac{21}{24}$, and multiply the numerator and denominator of $\frac{3}{6}$ by 4 to get $\frac{12}{24}$. Subtract the numerators, write the difference over the common denominator, and simplify: $\frac{21}{24} - \frac{12}{24} = \frac{9}{24} = \frac{3}{8}$.

Incorrect Answers:

- **A.** An error occurred when subtracting the numerators.
- **B.** The answer was not simplified.
- **C.** The wrong operation (addition) was used.

52. Correct Answer: A

Add the fraction of shorts that are white to the fraction of shorts that are navy blue to find the total amount of shorts that are either white or navy blue: $\frac{1}{3} + \frac{1}{5} = \frac{5}{15} + \frac{3}{15} = \frac{8}{15}$.

Incorrect Answers:

- **B.** No common denominator was found; the denominators were added together and the numerators were added together.
- **C.** The wrong operation (subtraction) was used.
- **D.** An error occurred when renaming $\frac{1}{3}$; $\frac{3}{15}$ was used as the equivalent fraction instead of $\frac{5}{15}$.

Adding and Subtracting Mixed Numbers *(page 48)*

53. Correct Answer: C

Subtract the number of laps Julia sprinted from the number of laps she jogged to find out how many more laps she jogged than sprinted: $4\frac{1}{4} - 2\frac{3}{4} = 3\frac{5}{4} - 2\frac{3}{4} = 1\frac{2}{4} = 1\frac{1}{2}$ laps.

Incorrect Answers:

- **A.** The wrong operation (addition) was used.
- **B.** The answer was not simplified.
- **D.** When $\frac{1}{4}$ was renamed as $\frac{5}{4}$, the whole number 4 was not changed to 3.

54. Correct Answer: C

Add to find how many doughnuts they sold all together. Find the least common denominator of the fractional part of the mixed numbers (6). $5\frac{5}{6}$ remains the same; rename $4\frac{2}{3}$ by multiplying the denominator and the numerator by 2 to get $4\frac{4}{6}$. Add the fractional parts of the mixed numbers first: $\frac{5}{6} + \frac{4}{6} = \frac{9}{6} = 1\frac{3}{6} = 1\frac{1}{2}$. Then add the whole numbers: $1 + 5 + 4 = 10$. The answer is $10\frac{1}{2}$ dozen.

Incorrect Answers:

- **A.** The answer was not simplified.
- **B.** The answer was not simplified.
- **D.** The wrong operation (subtraction) was used.

Explanations for Test B Answers *(cont.)*

55. Correct Answer: D
Subtract to find how much lemonade the guests drank. Find the least common denominator of the fractional part of the mixed numbers (12). Rename $6\frac{2}{4}$ by multiplying the denominator and the numerator by 3 to get $6\frac{6}{12}$; rename $3\frac{2}{3}$ by multiplying the denominator and the numerator by 4 to get $3\frac{8}{12}$. First, subtract the fractional parts of the mixed numbers, renaming $6\frac{6}{12}$ as $5\frac{18}{12}$: $\frac{18}{12} - \frac{8}{12} = \frac{10}{12} = \frac{5}{6}$. Then subtract the whole numbers: $5 - 3 = 2$. The answer is $2\frac{5}{6}$ gallons.
Incorrect Answers:
A. The answer was not simplified.
B. The fractional parts of the mixed numbers were subtracted in the wrong order. The numerator of the minuend was subtracted from the numerator of the subtrahend after finding the common denominators: $\frac{8}{12} - \frac{6}{12} = \frac{2}{12} = \frac{1}{6}$.
C. The wrong operation (addition) was used.

56. Correct Answer: B
Add the amount of grapes Osvaldo bought to the amount of strawberries to find the total amount of fruit he bought: $1\frac{3}{4} + 1\frac{5}{8} = 1\frac{6}{8} + 1\frac{5}{8} = 2\frac{11}{8} = 3\frac{3}{8}$ pounds.
Incorrect Answers:
A. An error occurred when simplifying $2\frac{11}{8}$.
C. The answer was not simplified.
D. A common denominator was not used, and the whole numbers, numerators, and denominators were added together.

Multiplying Fractions *(page 49)*

57. Correct Answer: C
Multiply the numerators ($3 \times 5 = 15$), multiply the denominators ($7 \times 6 = 42$), and simplify: $\frac{15}{42} = \frac{5}{14}$.
Incorrect Answers:
A. The fractions were cross-multiplied.
B. The answer was not simplified.
D. The fractions were cross-multiplied.

58. Correct Answer: A
Multiply the numerators ($2 \times 5 = 10$), multiply the denominators ($5 \times 8 = 40$), and simplify: $\frac{10}{40} = \frac{1}{4}$.
Incorrect Answers:
B. The denominators were multiplied, but the numerators were added.
C. The fractions were cross-multiplied.
D. The answer was not simplified completely.

59. Correct Answer: B
$\frac{2}{3}$ *of* the $\frac{3}{4}$ of all students that voted, voted for the winner. *Of* means multiply: $\frac{2}{3} \times \frac{3}{4} = \frac{6}{12} = \frac{1}{2}$.
Incorrect Answers:
A. The answer was not simplified.
C. The wrong operation (subtraction) was used.
D. The answer was not simplified.

60. Correct Answer: D
$\frac{1}{3}$ *of* the $\frac{3}{5}$ of students that play a sport play basketball. *Of* means multiply: $\frac{1}{3} \times \frac{3}{5} = \frac{3}{15} = \frac{1}{5}$.
Incorrect Answers:
A. The answer was not simplified.
B. The wrong operation (addition) was used.
C. The wrong operation (subtraction) was used.

Multiplying Fractions and Whole Numbers
(page 50)

61. Correct Answer: B
Write the whole number as an improper fraction ($\frac{32}{1}$). Multiply the numerators, multiply the denominators, and simplify: $\frac{32}{1} \times \frac{2}{8} = \frac{64}{8} = 8$.
Incorrect Answers:
A. 32 was renamed as $\frac{1}{32}$ instead of $\frac{32}{1}$.
C. The answer was not simplified.
D. 32 was renamed as $\frac{1}{32}$ instead of $\frac{32}{1}$, and the answer was not simplified.

62. Correct Answer: D
Laura's mom used $\frac{3}{4}$ *of* the 2-cup bag of powdered sugar. *Of* means multiply: $\frac{3}{4} \times 2$ cups $= \frac{3}{4} \times \frac{2}{1} = \frac{6}{4} = \frac{3}{2} = 1\frac{1}{2}$ cups.
Incorrect Answers:
A. The answer was not simplified.
B. The answer was not simplified.
C. 2 was renamed as $\frac{1}{2}$ instead of $\frac{2}{1}$.

63. Correct Answer: D
Of means multiply. $\frac{3}{5} \times 8 = \frac{3}{5} \times \frac{8}{1} = \frac{24}{5} = 4\frac{4}{5}$
Incorrect Answers:
A. The answer was not simplified.
B. 8 was renamed as $\frac{1}{8}$ instead of $\frac{8}{1}$.
C. The whole number and the numerator of the fraction were added, and the sum was written over the denominator.

64. Correct Answer: B
Juan has $\frac{2}{3}$ the number *of* customers that Haruo has. Multiply the number of customers Haruo has by $\frac{2}{3}$ to find out how many customers Juan has: $15 \times \frac{2}{3} = \frac{15}{1} \times \frac{2}{3} = \frac{30}{3} = 10$.
Incorrect Answers:
A. 15 is the number of customers Haruo has.
C. An error occurred when simplifying the answer ($\frac{30}{3} \neq 3$).
D. An error occurred when simplifying the answer ($\frac{30}{3} \neq 30$).

Dividing Fractions and Whole Numbers *(page 51)*

65. Correct Answer: B
Convert the whole number 4 to an improper fraction ($\frac{4}{1}$), change the division to multiplication, and change the divisor to its reciprocal ($\frac{1}{4}$): $\frac{2}{8} \times \frac{1}{4} = \frac{2}{32} = \frac{1}{16}$.
Incorrect Answers:
A. Division was changed to multiplication, but the reciprocal of $\frac{4}{1}$ ($\frac{1}{4}$) was not used.
C. The answer was not simplified.
D. The dividend was replaced with its reciprocal ($\frac{8}{2}$) instead of replacing the divisor (4) with its reciprocal.

66. Correct Answer: C
Divide the amount of gravel by the length of the driveway to find out how many tons of gravel is on each foot of the driveway: $\frac{3}{4} \div 6 = \frac{3}{4} \times \frac{1}{6} = \frac{3}{24} = \frac{1}{8}$.
Incorrect Answers:
A. Division was changed to multiplication, but the reciprocal of 6 was not used.
B. The answer was not simplified.
D. The dividend was replaced with its reciprocal ($\frac{4}{3}$) instead of replacing the divisor (6) with its reciprocal.

Explanations for Test B Answers (cont.)

67. **Correct Answer: C**
Convert the whole number 6 to an improper fraction ($\frac{6}{1}$), change the division to multiplication, and change the divisor to its reciprocal ($\frac{3}{2}$): $\frac{6}{1} \div \frac{2}{3} = \frac{6}{1} \times \frac{3}{2} = \frac{18}{2} = 9$.
Incorrect Answers:
- **A.** The answer was not simplified.
- **B.** The dividend was replaced with its reciprocal ($\frac{1}{6}$) instead of replacing the divisor ($\frac{2}{3}$) with its reciprocal.
- **D.** Division was changed to a multiplication, but the reciprocal of $\frac{2}{3}$ ($\frac{3}{2}$) was not used.

68. **Correct Answer: A**
Divide the amount of fertilizer he has by 2 (front yard and back yard) to find out how much fertilizer Osvaldo will put on the front yard: $\frac{3}{5} \div 2 = \frac{3}{5} \times \frac{1}{2} = \frac{3}{10}$.
Incorrect Answers:
- **B.** Division was changed to multiplication, but the reciprocal of $\frac{2}{1}$ ($\frac{1}{2}$) was not used.
- **C.** The dividend was replaced with its reciprocal ($\frac{5}{3}$) instead of replacing the divisor ($\frac{2}{1}$) with its reciprocal.
- **D.** Both the dividend and the divisor were replaced with their reciprocals.

Multiplying and Dividing Fractions to Solve Word Problems (page 52)

69. **Correct Answer: A**
Divide the amount of acres ($\frac{5}{8}$) set aside for spring flowers by the number of different kinds of spring flowers (3) to be planted to determine the number of acres that will have tulips planted on them: $\frac{5}{8} \div 3 = \frac{5}{8} \times \frac{1}{3} = \frac{5}{24}$.
Incorrect Answers:
- **B.** Division was changed to multiplication, but 3 was not replaced with its reciprocal.
- **C.** The divisor and the dividend were reversed.
- **D.** 3 was not replaced with its reciprocal, and the numerators and denominators were added.

70. **Correct Answer: D**
Divide the amount of fruit punch by the number of people who are sharing it (Mary and two friends = 3 people) to find out how much fruit punch each person will get: $\frac{3}{4} \div 3 = \frac{3}{4} \times \frac{1}{3} = \frac{3}{12} = \frac{1}{4}$ pitcher.
Incorrect Answers:
- **A.** The answer was not simplified.
- **B.** Division was changed to multiplication, but 3 was not replaced with its reciprocal.
- **C.** $\frac{3}{4}$ was divided by 2 instead of by 3.

71. **Correct Answer: C**
Multiply the number of loaves of bread Amir used on Friday (16) by the number of loaves he used on Saturday ($\frac{3}{4}$ as much) to find out how many loaves were used on Saturday: $\frac{3}{4} \times 16 = \frac{3}{4} \times \frac{16}{1} = \frac{48}{4} = 12$ loaves.
Incorrect Answers:
- **A.** The answer was not simplified.
- **B.** The answer was not simplified completely.
- **D.** 16 was divided by $\frac{3}{4}$ instead of being multiplied by it.

72. **Correct Answer: A**
The ponies get $\frac{1}{4}$ of the hay that the horses get. *Of* means multiply: $\frac{1}{4} \times \frac{3}{1} = \frac{3}{4}$.
Incorrect Answers:
- **B.** The wrong operation was used; the numerators were added and the denominators were added.
- **C.** The wrong operation was used; 3 was divided by $\frac{1}{4}$ instead of being multiplied.
- **D.** The fractions were cross multiplied.

Converting Measurement Units (page 53)

73. **Correct Answer: A**
10 mm = 1 cm, so 150 mm ÷ 10 mm per cm = 15 cm.
Incorrect Answers:
- **B.** 1 m = 1,000 mm, not 150 mm.
- **C.** An inch is a customary measurement and does not convert equally into metric units.
- **D.** 1,500 cm = 15,000 mm, not 150 mm.

74. **Correct Answer: D**
1 gal. = 4 qt., so 12 gal. × 4 qt. per gal. = 48 qt.
Incorrect Answers:
- **A.** 48 pt. = 6 gal., not 12 gal.
- **B.** 24 qt. = 6 gal., not 12 gal.
- **C.** 64 pt. = 8 gal., not 12 gal.

75. **Correct Answer: B**
1 mi. = 1,760 yd., so 14 mi. × 1,760 yd. per mile = 24,640 yd.
Incorrect Answers:
- **A.** 125 yd. and 10 ft. was calculated by dividing 1,760 yd. by 14 mi., instead of multiplying 1,760 yd. by 14 mi.
- **C.** 14,000 yd. was calculated by multiplying by 1,000 yd. per mi. instead of 1,760 yd. per mi.
- **D.** 73,920 yd. was calculated by multiplying 14 mi. by 5,280, which is the number of ft. in a mi., not the number of yd. in a mi.

76. **Correct Answer: C**
1,000 g = 1 kg, so 7,000 g ÷ 1,000 g per kg = 7 kg.
Incorrect Answers:
- **A.** 70 kg = 70,000 g, not 7,000 g.
- **B.** 7,000 kg = 7,000,000 g, not 7,000 g.
- **D.** 700 kg = 700,000 g, not 7,000 g.

Ordered Pairs (page 54)

77. **Correct Answer: D**
Move right 6 and up 4; there is a star.
Incorrect Answers:
- **A.** The diamond is located at (9,8).
- **B.** The circle is located at (7,3).
- **C.** The triangle is located at (4,6).

78. **Correct Answer: B**
Move right 8 and up 9; there is a square.
Incorrect Answers:
- **A.** The triangle is located at (4,6).
- **C.** The circle is located at (7,3).
- **D.** The diamond is located at (9,8).

79. Correct Answer: A
Point *E* is located 6 units to the right and 0 units above the origin: (6,0).
Incorrect Answers:
- **B.** Point *C* is located at (0,6).
- **C.** Point *D* is located at (9,5).
- **D.** Point *F* is located at (4,3).

80. Correct Answer: C
Point *A* is located 5 units to the right and 4 units above the origin: (5,4).
Incorrect Answers:
- **A.** Point *B* is located at (8,1).
- **B.** Point *F* is located at (4,3).
- **D.** Point *C* is located at (0,6).

Line Plots *(page 55)*

81. Correct Answer: C
The team drank 6 $\frac{1}{4}$ quarts of juice 6 times: ℍℍ I = 6 times.
Incorrect Answers:
- **A.** ℍℍ = 5 times, but the team drank 6 $\frac{1}{4}$ quarts of juice 6 times.
- **B.** IIII = 4 times, but the team drank 6 $\frac{1}{4}$ quarts of juice 6 times.
- **D.** ℍℍ II = 7 times, but the team drank 6 $\frac{1}{4}$ quarts of juice 6 times.

82. Correct Answer: C
10 $\frac{1}{2}$ quarts is the greatest, and 6 $\frac{1}{4}$ quarts is the least. Subtract to find the difference: 10 $\frac{1}{2}$ − 6 $\frac{1}{4}$ = 4 $\frac{1}{4}$ quarts.
Incorrect Answers:
- **A.** The wrong operation (addition) was used.
- **B.** The wrong value was used for the greatest quantity; 6 $\frac{1}{4}$ was subtracted from 9 $\frac{1}{2}$, instead of from 10 $\frac{1}{2}$.
- **D.** A subtraction error occurred.

83. Correct Answer: D
The team drank 7 $\frac{1}{8}$ quarts of juice 4 times, so there should be 4 Xs on the line plot.
Incorrect Answers:
- **A.** The team drank 7 $\frac{1}{8}$ quarts of juice 4 times, not 6.
- **B.** The team drank 7 $\frac{1}{8}$ quarts of juice 4 times, not 3.
- **C.** The team drank 7 $\frac{1}{8}$ quarts of juice 4 times, not 5.

84. Correct Answer: B
There are 22 tally marks, so the coach brought juice 22 times.
Incorrect Answers:
- **A.** 19 does not include the 3 times the team drank 8 $\frac{3}{4}$ quarts of juice.
- **C.** 17 does not include the 5 times the team drank 10 $\frac{1}{2}$ quarts of juice.
- **D.** 16 does not include the 6 times the team drank 6 $\frac{1}{4}$ quarts of juice.

Volume of Solid Figures *(page 56)*

85. Correct Answer: C
4 rows × 5 cubes in each row = 20 cubic units
Incorrect Answers:
- **A.** 29 cubic units was calculated by counting all the visible faces on the object.
- **B.** 15 cubic units was calculated by counting only 3 rows of the object.
- **D.** 25 cubic units was calculated by counting the faces on the top and the front of the object.

86. Correct Answer: A
The bottom layer has 6 cubes, the middle layer has 4 cubes, and the top layer has 2 cubes: 6 + 4 + 2 = 12 cubic units.
Incorrect Answers:
- **B.** 8 cubic units was calculated by adding the bottom (6) and top (2) layers of cubes; the middle layer (4) was not included.
- **C.** 21 cubic units was calculated by counting all the visible faces of the object.
- **D.** 10 cubic units was calculated by adding the bottom (6) and middle (4) layers of cubes; the top layer (2) was not included.

87. Correct Answer: B
6 cubes in each layer × 5 layers = 30 cubic units
Incorrect Answers:
- **A.** 41 cubic units was calculated by counting all the visible faces of the object.
- **C.** 25 cubic units would be 5 layers with 5 in each layer, instead of 6 in each layer.
- **D.** 24 cubic units included 4 layers, instead of 5 layers of cubes.

88. Correct Answer: B
6 cubes in each layer × 6 layers = 36 cubic units
Incorrect Answers:
- **A.** *Units* is the wrong label.
- **C.** 18 cubic units would be 6 layers with 3 cubes in each layer, instead of 6 cubes.
- **D.** 12 cubic units was calculated by adding 6 layers + 6 cubes, instead of multiplying 6 layers × 6 cubes.

Volume of Rectangular Prisms *(page 57)*

89. Correct Answer: A
$V = l \times w \times h$
10 cm × 5 cm × 8 cm = 400 cm³
Incorrect Answers:
- **B.** Cm is the wrong label.
- **C.** 23 cm³ was calculated by adding *l* + *w* + *h* instead of multiplying.
- **D.** 80 cm³ was calculated by multiplying *l* × *h*; *w* was not included.

90. Correct Answer: D
$V = l \times w \times h$
Volume of Rectangular Prism 1 = 4 yd. × 3 yd. × 3 yd. = 36 yd.³
Volume of Rectangular Prism 2 = 8 yd. × 5 yd. × 3 yd. = 120 yd.³
Total Volume = 36 yd.³ + 120 yd.³ = 156 yd.³
Incorrect Answers:
- **A.** yd.² is the wrong label.
- **B.** 29 yd.³ was calculated by adding all the numbers together instead of multiplying to find the volume of each rectangular prism separately and then adding the volumes together.
- **C.** 120 yd.³ is the volume of rectangular prism 2; it does not include the entire figure.

91. Correct Answer: C
$V = l \times w \times h$
12 in. × 3 in. × 7 in. = 252 in.³
Incorrect Answers:
- **A.** 21 in.³ was calculated by multiplying *w* × *h*; *l* was not included.
- **B.** 22 in.³ was calculated by adding *l* + *w* + *h* instead of multiplying.
- **D.** 84 in.3 was calculated by multiplying l × h; w was not included.

Explanations for Test B Answers *(cont.)*

92. Correct Answer: A
$V = l \times w \times h$
Volume of Rectangular Prism 1 = 5 m × 3 m × 4 m = 60 m³
Volume of Rectangular Prism 2 = 5 m × 4 m × 8 m = 160 m³
Total Volume = 60 m³ + 160 m³ = 220 m³
Incorrect Answers:
B. 120 m³ was calculated by using 8 m as the height in rectangular prism 1 instead of 4 m.
C. 100 m³ was calculated by subtracting the volume of rectangular prism 1 from the volume of rectangular prism 2 instead of adding the volumes together.
D. 160 m³ is the volume of rectangular prism 2; it does not include the entire figure.

Area of Rectangles with Fractional Sides (page 58)

93. Correct Answer: B
$A = l \times w$
Write the mixed numbers as improper fractions:
$\frac{21}{4} \times \frac{22}{3}$.
Cross cancel the numerator 21 with the denominator 3 and the numerator 22 with the denominator 4 to get
$\frac{7}{2} \times \frac{11}{1} = \frac{77}{2} = 38\frac{1}{2}$ sq. inches.
Incorrect Answers:
A. The answer was not simplified.
C. The mixed numbers were written as improper fractions, but the numerators were added together and the denominators were added together.
D. The whole numbers were multiplied, and then the fractions were multiplied.

94. Correct Answer: C
$A = l \times w$
Write the mixed numbers as improper fractions: $\frac{21}{10} \times \frac{17}{3}$.
Cross cancel the numerator 21 with the denominator 3
to get $\frac{7}{10} \times \frac{17}{1} = \frac{119}{10} = 11\frac{9}{10}$.
Incorrect Answers:
A. The whole numbers were multiplied, and then the fractions were multiplied and simplified.
B. The answer was not simplified.
D. The mixed numbers were written as improper fractions, but the numerators were added together and the denominators were added together.

95. Correct Answer: D
$A = l \times w$
Write the mixed numbers as improper fractions, then multiply:
$\frac{11}{2} \times \frac{15}{4} = \frac{165}{8} = 20\frac{5}{8}$ sq. inches.
Incorrect Answers:
A. The mixed numbers were written as improper fractions, but the numerators were added together and the denominators were added together.
B. The answer was not simplified.
C. The whole numbers were multiplied, and then the fractions were multiplied.

96. Correct Answer: A
$A = l \times w$
Write the mixed numbers as improper fractions:
$\frac{33}{5} \times \frac{50}{11}$.
Cross cancel the numerator 33 with the denominator 11 and the numerator 50 with the denominator 5 to get
$\frac{3}{1} \times \frac{10}{1} = \frac{30}{1} = 30$.
Incorrect Answers:
B. The mixed numbers were written as improper fractions, but the numerators were added together and the denominators were added together.
C. The answer was not simplified.
D. The whole numbers were multiplied, and then the fractions were multiplied.

Classifying Two-Dimensional Shapes (page 59)

97. Correct Answer: D
Rectangles are quadrilaterals with opposite sides parallel and four right angles. Squares are also quadrilaterals with opposite sides parallel and four right angles, so all squares are rectangles.
Incorrect Answers:
A. Squares have four sides of equal lengths, but rectangles do not. Therefore, all rectangles are not squares.
B. Trapezoids have only one set of parallel sides.
C. All rhombuses do not have four right angles.

98. Correct Answer: D
The two-dimensional figure is a square with four right angles and four equal sides.
Incorrect Answers:
A. The figure is a parallelogram with four equal sides, but it also has four right angles so this is not the best answer.
B. The figure has four equal sides, so it is not a rectangle.
C. The figure has four right angles, but *square* is a better description because it also has four equal sides.

99. Correct Answer: C
All rhombuses have four equal sides, but rectangles do not have four equal sides so this statement is false.
Incorrect Answers:
A. Quadrilaterals have four sides, and trapezoids have four sides so this statement is true.
B. Squares are parallelograms with four right angles, and rectangles are parallelograms with four right angles so this statement is true.
D. Rhombuses are parallelograms with four equal sides, and squares are parallelograms with four equal sides so this statement is true.

100. Correct Answer: B
The figure has four sides (quadrilateral), has opposite sides parallel and equal length (parallelogram), and has four right angles (rectangle).
Incorrect Answers:
A. The figure is a quadrilateral and a parallelogram, but not a rhombus because it does not have four equal sides.
C. The figure is a quadrilateral and a rectangle, but not a square because it does not have four equal sides.
D. The figure is a quadrilateral and a parallelogram, but not a trapezoid because it has four right angles and two sets of parallel sides.

Explanations for Test C Answers

Multiplying Multi-Digit Numbers *(page 60)*

1. Correct Answer: B
112 space ships × 25 aliens per ship = 2,800 aliens
Incorrect Answers:
A. A regrouping error occurred in the hundreds column when adding the partial products.
C. 112 was multiplied by 2 ones instead of by 2 tens. (The 2 in 25 is worth 2 tens.)
D. An error occurred in the hundreds column when adding the partial products.

2. Correct Answer: A
Follow steps 1–6.
1. Write 29 under 309. **2.** Multiply 309 by 9 ones to get 2,781 (remember to regroup). **3.** Write the partial product (2,781).
4. Multiply 309 by 2 tens to get 6,180 (remember to regroup).
5. Write the partial product (6,180).
6. Add the partial products: 2,781 + 6,180 = 8,961.
Incorrect Answers:
B. A regrouping error occurred in the hundreds column when adding the partial products.
C. 309 was multiplied by 2 ones instead of by 2 tens. (The 2 in 29 is worth 2 tens.)
D. An error occurred in the tens column when adding the partial products.

3. Correct Answer: C
Perimeter of a square = $4s$: $P = 4 \times 16 = 64$ ft.
Incorrect Answers:
A. The length of one side of the shed was multiplied by another side of the shed; this is the area of the shed.
B. A regrouping error occurred in the tens column when multiplying 16 × 4.
D. A multiplication error occurred in the ones column when multiplying 16 × 4.

4. Correct Answer: D
Follow steps 1–6. **1.** Write 72 under 96. **2.** Multiply 96 by 2 ones to get 192 (remember to regroup). **3.** Write the partial product (192). **4.** Multiply 96 by 7 tens to get 6,720 (remember to regroup). **5.** Write the partial product (6,720).
6. Add the partial products: 192 + 6,720 = 6,912.
Incorrect Answers:
A. A regrouping error occurred in the hundreds place when adding the partial products.
B. 96 was multiplied by 7 ones instead of by 7 tens. (The 7 in 72 is worth 72.)
C. An addition error occurred in the tens column when adding the partial products.

Dividing by Two-digit Divisors *(page 61)*

5. Correct Answer: D
Divide the amount of money the club has by the cost of each ticket to find out how many tickets they can buy: 168 ÷ 14 = 12.
Incorrect Answers:
A. An error occurred when dividing 28 by 14 in the second division step: 28 ÷ 14 ≠ 7 because 7 × 14 = 98 and 98 is greater than 28.
B. An error occurred when dividing 28 by 14 in the second division step: 28 ÷ 14 ≠ 4 because 4 × 14 = 56 and 56 is greater than 28.
C. An error occurred when dividing 28 by 14 in the second division step: 28 ÷ 14 ≠ 1 because 1 × 14 = 14, leaving room for 14 to go into 28 one more time.

6. Correct Answer: C
The first digit of the dividend (8) is less than the divisor (16), so divide 16 into the first two digits (84).
DIVIDE: 84 ÷ 16 = 5. Write 5 in the quotient above 4.
MULTIPLY: 5 × 16 = 80.
SUBTRACT: 84 – 80 = 4. 4 is the number *left over* after dividing (remainder). The *quotient* is 5 R4.
Incorrect Answers:
A. The remainder (20) is greater than the divisor, which indicates that the quotient is incorrect.
B. 16 does not go into 84 six times because 6 × 16 = 96, and 96 is greater than 84.
D. The remainder was not included in the answer.

7. Correct Answer: B
Divide the number of new books by the number books that fit on each shelf to find out how many shelves are needed:
196 ÷ 14 = 14.
Incorrect Answers:
A. An error occurred when dividing 56 by 14 in the second division step: 56 ÷ 14 ≠ 9 because 9 × 14 = 126 and 126 is greater than 56.
C. An error occurred when dividing 56 by 14 in the second division step: 56 ÷ 14 ≠ 3 because 3 × 14 = 42, leaving room for 14 to go into 56 one more time.
D. An error occurred when dividing 56 by 14 in the second division step: 56 ÷ 14 ≠ 5 because 5 × 14 = 70 and 70 is greater than 56.

8. Correct Answer: B
The divisor (35) is greater than the first digit in the dividend (7), so divide 35 into the first two digits of the dividend (76).
DIVIDE: 76 ÷ 35 = 2. Write 2 in the quotient above 6.
MULTIPLY: 2 × 35 =70. *SUBTRACT:* 76 – 70 = 6.
BRING DOWN: the 8 from the ones column of the dividend to form 68.
DIVIDE: 68 ÷ 35 = 1. Write 1 in the quotient above 8.
MULTIPLY: 1 × 35 = 35. *SUBTRACT:* 68 – 35 = 33. There is nothing left to bring down; 33 is the number *left over* after dividing (remainder). The *quotient* is 21 R33.
Incorrect Answers:
A. A subtraction error occurred after dividing 68 by 35: 68 – 35 ≠ 23.
C. An error occurred when dividing 68 by 35 in the second division step: 68 ÷ 35 ≠ 2 because 2 × 35 = 70, and 70 is greater than 68. A subtraction error followed: 68 – 70 ≠ 2.
D. The remainder (68) is greater than the divisor, which indicates that the quotient is incorrect.

Reading and Writing Decimals to Thousandths *(page 62)*

9. Correct Answer: D
8,000 + 100 + 40 + 5 + 0.5 + 0.03 + 0.009 = 8,145.539
Incorrect Answers:
A. This is $\frac{5}{100} + \frac{3}{1,000} + \frac{9}{10,000}$ instead of $\frac{5}{10} + \frac{3}{100} + \frac{9}{1,000}$.
B. This is 80,000 instead of 8,000.
C. This is 80,000 + 1,000 instead of 8,000 + 100.

10. Correct Answer: C
3 × 10,000 + 7 × 1,000 + 2 × 100 + 8 × 10 + 1 × 1 + 4 × $\frac{1}{10}$ = 30,000 + 7,000 + 200 + 80 + 1 + 0.4 = 37,281.4
Incorrect Answers:
A. This is 37,281.04.
B. This is 307,281.4.
D. This is 37,290.4.

Explanations for Test C Answers *(cont.)*

11. Correct Answer: C
And indicates where the decimal point belongs.
Incorrect Answers:
- **A.** This is two and nine hundred sixty-eight ten thousandths.
- **B.** This is two thousand nine hundred sixty-eight ten thousandths.
- **D.** This is two and nine hundred sixty-eight hundred thousandths.

12. Correct Answer: A
sixty-seven thousand thirty-three and ninety-four hundredths =
67,000 + 33 + 0.94 = 67,033.94
Incorrect Answers:
- **B.** *Thirty-three hundred* = 3,300. 67,000 + 3,300 + 0.94 = 70,300.94
- **C.** This is 6,733.94.
- **D.** This is 67,033.094.

Interpreting Place Value *(page 63)*

13. Correct Answer: D
$3.027 = 3\frac{27}{1,000}$
$3.027 =$ three and twenty-seven thousandths $= 3\frac{27}{1,000}$
Incorrect Answers:
- **A.** $3\frac{27}{10} = 5.7$
- **B.** $3\frac{27}{100} = 3.27$
- **C.** $\frac{327}{1,000} = 0.327$

14. Correct Answer: D
$6\frac{9}{10} =$ six and nine tenths $= 6.9$
Incorrect Answers:
- **A.** $6.009 = 6\frac{9}{1,000}$
- **B.** $6.09 = 6\frac{9}{100}$
- **C.** $0.69 = \frac{69}{100}$

15. Correct Answer: C
The 6 in 332,654 is worth 6 hundreds or 600. The 6 in 362,354 is worth 6 ten thousands or 60,000. $600 \times 100 = 60,000$, so the 6 in 332,654 is worth 100 times less than the value of the 6 in 362,354.
Incorrect Answers:
- **A.** The 6 in 332,654 is two *places* to the right of the 6 in 362,354, but each place value is worth 10 times less than the place value to its left.
- **B.** The value of the number 10 times less than 60,000 is 6,000, not 600.
- **D.** The value of the number 1,000 times less than 60,000 is 60, not 600.

16. Correct Answer: B
$0.03 \times 100 = 3.0$
Incorrect Answers:
- **A.** 30.0 is 1,000 times greater than 0.03.
- **C.** 0.3 is 10 times greater than 0.03.
- **D.** 0.0003 is 100 times less than 0.03.

Comparing Decimals to Thousandths *(page 64)*

17. Correct Answer: B
Shirley drank the most juice: $1.\underline{2} > 1.\underline{0}2$ and $1.\underline{2} > 1.\underline{0}02$.
Incorrect Answers:
- **A.** Jim drank the least amount of juice:
  $1.\underline{0}02 < 1.\underline{2}$ and $1.0\underline{0}2 < 1.0\underline{2}$.
- **C.** Jerry did not drink the most juice: $1.\underline{0}2 < 1.\underline{2}$.
- **D.** $1.2\mathit{00} \neq 1.02\mathit{0} \neq 1.002$

18. Correct Answer: D
Ignore the decimal points to compare:
$3.\underline{2}34 < 3.\underline{4}30 < 3.\underline{5}00 < 3.\underline{5}67$.
Incorrect Answers:
- **A.** 2.562, 2.532, 2.522, 2.51 are in order from greatest to least, not least to greatest.
- **B.** 0.7 is the least decimal; the order should be: 0.7, 0.741, 0.75, 0.8.
- **C.** The order should be: 0.003, 0.02, 0.1, 1.01.

19. Correct Answer: A
2.189 comes between 2.185 and 2.19: 2.1$\underline{8}$5, 2.1$\underline{8}$9, 2.19$\mathit{0}$.
Incorrect Answers:
- **B.** 2.1$\underline{8}$3 comes before 2.1$\underline{8}$5.
- **C.** 2.1$\underline{9}$1 comes after 2.19$\mathit{0}$.
- **D.** 2.1$\underline{8}\mathit{0}$ comes before 2.1$\underline{8}$5.

20. Correct Answer: C
5.721 > 5.82 is not true; $5.\underline{7}21 < 5.\underline{8}2$.
Incorrect Answers:
- **A.** 0.43 = 0.430 is true.
- **B.** $1.\underline{9}8 > 1.\underline{8}9$ is true.
- **D.** $3.7\underline{0} < 3.7\underline{4}$ is true.

Rounding Decimals *(page 65)*

21. Correct Answer: B
To round to the nearest tenth, look at the digit to the right of the tenths place. The digit (2) is less than 5, so round down.
Incorrect Answers:
- **A.** 238.928 was rounded to the nearest hundredth.
- **C.** 238.928 was rounded to the nearest one.
- **D.** 238.928 was rounded incorrectly to the nearest hundredth.

22. Correct Answer: A
To round to the nearest hundred dollars, look at the digit to the right of the hundreds place. The digit (4) is less than 5, so round down.
Incorrect Answers:
- **B.** $145.78 was incorrectly rounded up.
- **C.** $145.78 was rounded to the nearest one dollar.
- **D.** $145.78 was rounded to the nearest tenth or nearest ten cents.

23. Correct Answer: D
15.3724 rounds down to 15.372 because the digit to the right of the thousandths place (4) is less than 5.
Incorrect Answers:
- **A.** 15.3711 rounded to the nearest thousandth = 15.371.
- **B.** 15.3713 rounded to the nearest thousandth = 15.371.
- **C.** 15.3726 rounded to the nearest thousandth = 15.373.

24. Correct Answer: C
To round to the nearest ten, look at the digit to the right of the tens place. The digit (3) is less than 5, so round down.
Incorrect Answers:
- **A.** 153.552 was rounded to the nearest tenth.
- **B.** 153.552 was rounded to the nearest one.
- **D.** 153.552 was rounded to the nearest hundred.

Adding and Subtracting Decimals *(page 66)*

25. Correct Answer: D
Align the decimal points before subtracting:
53.3 − 29.58 = 23.72.

Explanations for Test C Answers (cont.)

25. Incorrect Answers:
   A. The decimal is in the wrong place.
   B. The wrong operation (addition) was used.
   C. The decimal points were not aligned before subtracting; the numbers were aligned flush right.

26. Correct Answer: A
   Align the decimal points before adding: $16.78 + 75.4 = 92.18$.
   Incorrect Answers:
   B. The decimal points were not aligned before adding; the numbers were aligned flush right.
   C. The decimal points were not aligned before adding; the numbers were aligned flush right.
   D. The decimal is in the wrong place.

27. Correct Answer: C
   Add to find how much the cans weighed all together: $93.4 + 92.92 = 186.32$ g.
   Incorrect Answers:
   A. The wrong operation (subtraction) was used.
   B. The decimal points were not aligned before adding; the numbers were aligned flush right.
   D. The decimal is in the wrong place.

28. Correct Answer: C
   Subtract to find the difference: $40.10 - 36.37 = 3.73$ yd.
   Incorrect Answers:
   A. A *0* was not written after 40.1, so the 7 from 36.37 was just brought down into the answer.
   B. The decimal is in the wrong place.
   D. The wrong operation (addition) was used.

Multiplying and Dividing Decimals (page 67)

29. Correct Answer: C
   $46.86 \div 2.2 = 21.3$
   Incorrect Answers:
   A. The decimal is in the wrong place.
   B. The wrong operation (subtraction) was used.
   D. The decimal is in the wrong place.

30. Correct Answer: D
   $7.08 \times 8.7 = 61.596$
   Incorrect Answers:
   A. The decimal is in the wrong place.
   B. When multiplying 7.08 by 8, *0* was not written as a placeholder in the partial product.
   C. The decimal is in the wrong place.

31. Correct Answer: D
   To find out how much meat Dyana ate each day, divide: $15.6 \div 5.2 = 3.0$ ounces per day.
   Incorrect Answers:
   A. The decimal is in the wrong place.
   B. The wrong operation (multiplication) was used.
   C. *Days* is the wrong label.

32. Correct Answer: B
   602.65 grams $\times$ 5 fishing poles = 3,013.25 grams
   Incorrect Answers:
   A. The wrong operation was used; the weight of each pole was divided by 5.
   C. The decimal is in the wrong place.
   D. 602.65 was multiplied by 4 fishing poles instead of 5.

Multiple-step Problems with Decimals (page 68)

33. Correct Answer: D
   The weight of the marbles Carl had left after he gave some marbles to his brother is needed; that amount will be divided by 4 to get the final answer.
   Incorrect Answers:
   A. *The large bag weighed 1.42 kilograms* is needed to solve step 1, but it is a given fact; it does not need to be found.
   B. The number of marbles in the bags is not relevant to the problem; the problem is about the weight of the marbles.
   C. *Carl gave his brother 0.30 kilograms of marbles* is needed to solve step 1, but it is a given fact; it does not need to be found.

34. Correct Answer: B
   Subtraction is used to find the weight of the marbles Carl had left after giving some to his brother.
   Incorrect Answers:
   A. Addition is used to find the total; it does not tell how much is left.
   C. Division is used to divide quantities into equal groups.
   D. Multiplication is used to find the total amount in equal groups.

35. Correct Answer: A
   Equally separated is a clue for division.
   Incorrect Answers:
   B. *How much* does not suggest a particular operation.
   C. *The smaller bags* is not a clue to indicate what operation to use.
   D. *Took 0.30 kilograms of marbles* is a clue to help choose the operation in step one.

36. Correct Answer: C
   1.42 kg of marbles – 0.30 kg of marbles = 1.12 kg of marbles; 1.12 kilograms $\div$ 4 bags = 0.28 kilograms per bag
   Incorrect Answers:
   A. *Bags of marbles* is the wrong label.
   B. *1.12 kilograms* is what Carl had left after he gave his brother 0.30 kilograms from the large bag.
   D. *0.355 kilograms* was calculated by dividing 1.42 kilograms by 4 bags; the marbles that Carl gave to his brother were not subtracted.

Simplifying Expressions (page 69)

37. Correct Answer: B
   $(5^2 + 5) \times (30 \div 10) - 2 = (25 + 5) \times 3 - 2 = 30 \times 3 - 2 = 90 - 2 = 88$
   Incorrect Answers:
   A. 5^2 was calculated as $5 \times 2 = 10$ instead of 5×5.
   C. 2 was not subtracted in the last step.
   D. 5^2 was calculated as $5 + 2 = 7$ instead of 5×5.

38. Correct Answer: A
   $(2 + 3) \times (12 \div 4) + 3 = 5 \times 3 + 3 = 18$, not 45.
   Incorrect Answers:
   B. $4 + (45 \times 0) - 3 = 4 + 0 - 3 = 1$
   C. $81 \div (3 + 2 + 4) \times 3 = 81 \div 9 \times 3 = 9 \times 3 = 27$
   D. $(7 \times 2) + (6 - 3) + 2 = 14 + 3 + 2 = 19$

39. Correct Answer: C
   $(56 \div 8) \times (48 \div 8) + 10^2 = 7 \times 6 + 100 = 42 + 100 = 142$
   Incorrect Answers:
   A. 100 was not added in the last step.
   B. 10^2 was calculated as $10 \times 2 = 20$ instead of 10×10.
   D. 10^2 was calculated as $10 + 2 = 12$ instead of 10×10.

Explanations for Test C Answers *(cont.)*

40. Correct Answer: D
$(8 \times 3) \div (8 - n) + 6^2 = (8 \times 3) \div (8 - 6) + 6^2 = 24 \div 2 + 36 =$
$12 + 36 = 48$
Incorrect Answers:
- **A.** 6^2 was not simplified to 36; instead of adding $12 + 36$ in the last step $12 + 6$ was added.
- **B.** 6 was not substituted for n; $- n$ was omitted from the problem.
- **C.** 6^2 was not simplified to 36; it was simplified to 6. Then $2 + 6$ was added before dividing $24 \div 2$.

Using Parentheses and Brackets *(page 70)*

41. Correct Answer: A
$[95 - (12 \times 7)] + 9^3 = [95 - 84] + 729 = 11 + 729 = 740$
Incorrect Answers:
- **B.** The order of operations was not followed; the first step should be (12×7), but it was $95 - 12$.
- **C.** 9^3 was calculated as $9 \times 3 = 27$ instead of $9 \times 9 \times 9$.
- **D.** 11 was not added in the last step.

42. Correct Answer: C
$3 + [(6.31 \times 2.4) + (28.7 \div 4.1)] \times 2 = 3 + [15.144 + 7] \times 2 =$
$3 + 22.144 \times 2 = 3 + 44.288 = 47.288$
Incorrect Answers:
- **A.** The order of operations was not followed; after simplifying inside the brackets, the result (22.144) was added to 3 before being multiplied by 2.
- **B.** 3 was not added in the last step.
- **D.** $\times 2$ was omitted from the problem.

43. Correct Answer: B
$[(18 \div w) \times (8 + 3)] - 17 = [(18 \div 9) \times (8 + 3)] - 17 =$
$[2 \times 11] - 17 = 22 - 17 = 5$
Incorrect Answers:
- **A.** The order of operations was not followed; after dividing $18 \div 9 = 2$, 2 was multiplied by 8 instead of adding $8 + 3$ first.
- **C.** A division error occurred; $18 \div 9$ was calculated as 9 instead of 2.
- **D.** 17 was not subtracted in the last step.

44. Correct Answer: A
$246 - [(55 + 13) + (2^2 \times 6)] = 246 - [68 + (4 \times 6)] =$
$246 - [68 + 24] = 246 - 92 = 154$
Incorrect Answers:
- **B.** The order of operations was not followed; 68 was subtracted from 246 before it was added to 24.
- **C.** 92 was not subtracted from 246 in the last step.
- **D.** 2^2 was calculated as 2 instead of $2 \times 2 = 4$.

Finding Common Denominators *(page 71)*

45. Correct Answer: C
List the multiples of the denominators (4 and 8), then use the *least common* multiple (8) as the common denominator. $\frac{3}{8}$ remains the same; rename $\frac{3}{4}$ by multiplying the numerator and denominator by 2 to get $\frac{6}{8}$.
Incorrect Answers:
- **A.** The correct common denominator was used for $\frac{3}{4}$, but the numerator remained the same $(\frac{3}{8})$.
- **B.** The correct common denominator was used, but the numerator of $\frac{3}{4}$ was replaced by the factor used to get the common denominator.
- **D.** The denominator of $\frac{3}{4}$ was correctly changed to 8, but the numerator was incorrectly changed to 4.

46. Correct Answer: A
List the multiples of the denominators (3 and 18), then use the *least common* multiple (18) as the common denominator. Rename both fractions using the common denominator 18. Multiply the numerator and the denominator of $\frac{2}{3}$ by 6 to get $\frac{12}{18}$; $\frac{5}{18}$ remains the same.
Incorrect Answers:
- **B.** The correct denominator (18) was used to rename $\frac{2}{3}$, but the numerator of the fraction was replaced by the factor used to get the common denominator.
- **C.** The correct common denominator was used, but the numerator of $\frac{2}{3}$ was not renamed.
- **D.** The correct common denominator was used, but the numerator of $\frac{2}{3}$ was incorrectly changed to 3.

47. Correct Answer: D
List the multiples of the denominators (3 and 2), then use the *least common* multiple (6) as the common denominator. Rename the fractions using 6 as the common denominator. Multiply the numerator and denominator of $\frac{2}{3}$ by 2 to get $\frac{4}{6}$, and multiply the numerator and denominator of $\frac{1}{2}$ by 3 to get $\frac{3}{6}$.
Incorrect Answers:
- **A.** A common denominator was found by adding the two denominators together, and the numerators remained the same.
- **B.** The correct common denominator was used, but the numerators were not renamed.
- **C.** The correct common denominator was used, but the numerators of the fractions were replaced by the factors used to get the common denominator of each of the fractions.

48. Correct Answer: B
List the multiples of the denominators (6 and 4), then use the *least common* multiple of the denominators (12) as the common denominator. Rename the fractions using 12 as the common denominator. Multiply the numerator and denominator of $\frac{5}{6}$ by 2 to get $\frac{10}{12}$, and multiply the numerator and denominator of $\frac{3}{4}$ by 3 to get $\frac{9}{12}$.
Incorrect Answers:
- **A.** The correct common denominator was used, but the numerators of the fractions were replaced by the factors used to get the common denominator of each of the fractions.
- **C.** 6 is not a common denominator for 6 and 4, because 6 is not a multiple of the denominator 4.
- **D.** The correct common denominator was used, but the numerators were not renamed.

Adding and Subtracting Fractions with Unlike Denominators *(page 72)*

49. Correct Answer: C
Add the fraction of chocolate sundaes sold to the fraction of strawberry sundaes sold to find the fraction of sundaes that were either strawberry or chocolate: $\frac{2}{4} + \frac{1}{3} = \frac{6}{12} + \frac{4}{12} = \frac{10}{12} = \frac{5}{6}$.
Incorrect Answers:
- **A.** The answer was not simplified.
- **B.** The wrong operation (subtraction) was used.
- **D.** The numerators were added together, and the denominators were added together.

Explanations for Test C Answers *(cont.)*

50. Correct Answer: A
Add to find how much rope John has all together. Find the least common denominator of the two fractions (21). Rename $\frac{3}{7}$ by multiplying the denominator and the numerator by 3 to get $\frac{9}{21}$; $\frac{6}{21}$ remains the same. Add the numerators, write the sum over the common denominator, and simplify: $\frac{9}{21} + \frac{6}{21} = \frac{15}{21} = \frac{5}{7}$.
Incorrect Answers:
- **B.** The answer was not simplified.
- **C.** The wrong operation (subtraction) was used.
- **D.** The numerators were added together, and the denominators were added together.

51. Correct Answer: D
Subtract to find how much more gasoline Nicholas bought on Saturday: $\frac{3}{4} - \frac{2}{8} = \frac{6}{8} - \frac{2}{8} = \frac{4}{8} = \frac{1}{2}$.
Incorrect Answers:
- **A.** The answer was not simplified.
- **B.** The answer was not simplified completely.
- **C.** The wrong operation (addition) was used.

52. Correct Answer: B
Subtract to find how much jam Margaret will have left. Find the least common denominator of the fractions (24), and rename both fractions using the common denominator. Rename $\frac{4}{6}$ by multiplying the denominator and numerator by 4 to get $\frac{16}{24}$, and rename $\frac{2}{8}$ by multiplying the numerator and denominator by 3 to get $\frac{6}{24}$. Subtract the numerators, write the difference over the common denominator, and simplify: $\frac{16}{24} - \frac{6}{24} = \frac{10}{24} = \frac{5}{12}$.
Incorrect Answers:
- **A.** The numerators were added together, the denominators were added together, and the result was simplified.
- **C.** The answer was not simplified.
- **D.** The wrong operation (addition) was used.

Adding and Subtracting Mixed Numbers *(page 73)*

53. Correct Answer: A
Subtract the number of miles Michael drove from the number of miles Andrew drove to find out how much farther Andrew drove: $21\frac{2}{5} - 15\frac{1}{15} = 21\frac{6}{15} - 15\frac{1}{15} = 6\frac{5}{15} = 6\frac{1}{3}$.
Incorrect Answers:
- **B.** The answer was not simplified.
- **C.** A subtraction error occurred in the ones column.
- **D.** The numerators of the fractional parts of the mixed numbers were added.

54. Correct Answer: B
Add to find how much fabric Claudia used in all:
$5\frac{3}{5} + 4\frac{1}{2} = 5\frac{6}{10} + 4\frac{5}{10} = 9\frac{11}{10} = 10\frac{1}{10}$.
Incorrect Answers:
- **A.** The answer was not simplified.
- **C.** The wrong operation (subtraction) was used.
- **D.** The numerators of the fractions in the mixed numbers were added together, the denominators of the fractions in the mixed numbers were added together, and the whole numbers were added together.

55. Correct Answer: D
Add to find the total number bags of fertilizer Kako used:
$3\frac{4}{10} + 2\frac{2}{3} = 3\frac{12}{30} + 2\frac{20}{30} = 5\frac{32}{30} = 6\frac{2}{30} = 6\frac{1}{15}$.
Incorrect Answers:
- **A.** The answer was not simplified completely.
- **B.** The numerators of the fractions in the mixed numbers were added together, the denominators of the fractions in

the mixed numbers were added together, and the whole numbers were added together.
- **C.** When simplifying $5\frac{32}{30}$, the whole number 1 from $\frac{32}{30}$ was not added to 5.

56. Correct Answer: C
Subtract to find the difference between the pizza ordered and the pizza that was left: $7 - 3\frac{4}{12} = 6\frac{12}{12} - 3\frac{4}{12} = 3\frac{8}{12} = 3\frac{2}{3}$.
Incorrect Answers:
- **A.** The answer was not simplified.
- **B.** The answer was not simplified completely.
- **D.** When renaming 7 to a mixed number, 7 was not reduced to 6.

Multiplying Fractions *(page 74)*

57. Correct Answer: B
Multiply the numerators ($3 \times 2 = 6$), multiply the denominators ($5 \times 6 = 30$), and simplify: $\frac{6}{30} = \frac{1}{5}$.
Incorrect Answers:
- **A.** An error occurred when simplifying the product ($\frac{6}{30}$).
- **C.** The answer was not simplified.
- **D.** The fractions were cross-multiplied to get $\frac{10}{18}$ and then simplified.

58. Correct Answer: D
Multiply the numerators ($8 \times 3 = 24$), multiply the denominators ($9 \times 4 = 36$), and simplify: $\frac{24}{36} = \frac{2}{3}$.
Incorrect Answers:
- **A.** The answer was not simplified.
- **B.** The fractions were cross-multiplied.
- **C.** The answer was not simplified completely.

59. Correct Answer: C
Multiply the number of candles Wanda sold by $\frac{1}{4}$ to find out how many candles Judy sold: $\frac{1}{4} \times \frac{2}{3} = \frac{2}{12} = \frac{1}{6}$.
Incorrect Answers:
- **A.** The answer was not simplified.
- **B.** The wrong operation (addition) was used.
- **D.** The fractions were cross-multiplied.

60. Correct Answer: A
Mary will use $\frac{1}{2}$ of the amount of apples the recipe requires. *Of* means multiply: $\frac{1}{2} \times \frac{5}{8} = \frac{5}{16}$.
Incorrect Answers:
- **B.** The denominators were added together, and the numerators were added together.
- **C.** The fractions were cross-multiplied to get $\frac{8}{10}$ and then simplified.
- **D.** The wrong operation (addition) was used.

Multiplying Fractions and Whole Numbers *(page 75)*

61. Correct Answer: D
Write the whole number as an improper fraction ($\frac{15}{1}$). Multiply the numerators, multiply the denominators, and simplify: $\frac{2}{3} \times \frac{15}{1} = \frac{30}{3} = 10$.
Incorrect Answers:
- **A.** The wrong operation (addition) was used.
- **B.** 15 was replaced with $\frac{1}{15}$ instead of $\frac{15}{1}$.
- **C.** The answer was not simplified.

62. Correct Answer: C
Multiply the number of jars of blueberry preserves by $\frac{2}{3}$ to find out how many jars of blackberry preserves the Walker family made: $\frac{12}{1} \times \frac{2}{3} = \frac{24}{3} = 8$.

62. Incorrect Answers:
 A. An error occurred when simplifying the answer ($\frac{24}{3} \neq 6$).
 B. 12 was replaced with $\frac{1}{12}$ instead of $\frac{12}{1}$.
 D. The answer was not simplified.

63. Correct Answer: C
Write the whole number as an improper fraction ($\frac{20}{1}$). Multiply the numerators, multiply the denominators, and simplify: $\frac{20}{1} \times \frac{5}{8} = \frac{100}{8} = 12\frac{4}{8} = 12\frac{1}{2}$.
Incorrect Answers:
 A. 20 was replaced with $\frac{1}{20}$ instead of $\frac{20}{1}$.
 B. The whole number and the numerator were added; the sum was placed over the denominator and simplified.
 D. The answer was not simplified.

64. Correct Answer: B
14 batches $\times \frac{3}{8}$ cup per batch $= \frac{14}{1} \times \frac{3}{8} = \frac{42}{8} = \frac{21}{4} = 5\frac{1}{4}$
Incorrect Answers:
 A. The answer was not simplified.
 C. The whole number and the numerator were added; the sum was placed over the denominator and simplified.
 D. An error occurred when simplifying the answer ($\frac{42}{8} \neq 5$).

Dividing Fractions and Whole Numbers (page 76)

65. Correct Answer: D
Convert the whole number 3 to an improper fraction ($\frac{3}{1}$), change the division to multiplication, and change the divisor to its reciprocal ($\frac{10}{5}$): $\frac{3}{1} \times \frac{10}{5} = \frac{30}{5} = 6$.
Incorrect Answers:
 A. The answer was not simplified.
 B. Division was changed to multiplication, but the reciprocal of $\frac{5}{10}$ ($\frac{10}{5}$) was not used.
 C. The dividend ($\frac{3}{1}$) was replaced with its reciprocal instead of replacing the divisor ($\frac{5}{10}$) with its reciprocal.

66. Correct Answer: A
Divide the $\frac{1}{2}$ gallon of punch that Jackie made by the 6 glasses to find how much punch to put in each glass:
$\frac{1}{2} \div 6 = \frac{1}{2} \times \frac{1}{6} = \frac{1}{12}$ gallon.
Incorrect Answers:
 B. Both $\frac{1}{2}$ and $\frac{6}{1}$ were changed to their reciprocals before multiplying.
 C. Division was changed to multiplication, but the reciprocal of $\frac{6}{1}$ ($\frac{1}{6}$) was not used.
 D. The dividend and the divisor were reversed.

67. Correct Answer: B
Convert the whole number 3 to an improper fraction ($\frac{3}{1}$), change the division to multiplication, and change the divisor to its reciprocal ($\frac{1}{3}$): $\frac{3}{5} \times \frac{1}{3} = \frac{3}{15} = \frac{1}{5}$.
Incorrect Answers:
 A. An error occurred when simplifying the answer ($\frac{3}{15}$).
 C. The answer was not simplified.
 D. Division was changed to multiplication, but the reciprocal of $\frac{3}{1}$ ($\frac{1}{3}$) was not used.

68. Correct Answer: C
Divide the amount of meatloaf left over by the number of family members eating meatloaf to find how much meatloaf each family member will receive: $\frac{3}{4} \div 4 = \frac{3}{4} \times \frac{1}{4} = \frac{3}{16}$.
Incorrect Answers:
 A. Division was changed to multiplication, but the reciprocal of 4 ($\frac{1}{4}$) was not used.
 B. Both $\frac{3}{4}$ and 4 were changed to their reciprocals before multiplying.
 D. The dividend ($\frac{3}{4}$) was replaced with its reciprocal instead of replacing the divisor (4) with it's reciprocal.

Multiplying and Dividing Fractions to Solve Word Problems (page 77)

69. Correct Answer: C
Divide the weight of the butter by 3 parts to find the weight of each part: $\frac{1}{2} \div 3 = \frac{1}{2} \times \frac{1}{3} = \frac{1}{6}$ lb. per part.
Incorrect Answers:
 A. Division was changed to multiplication, but the reciprocal of 3 ($\frac{1}{3}$) was not used.
 B. Both $\frac{1}{2}$ and 3 were replaced with their reciprocals.
 D. The dividend ($\frac{1}{2}$) and the divisor (3) were reversed.

70. Correct Answer: B
Divide the amount of clay by the number of classrooms to find out how much clay each classroom will receive: $\frac{4}{6}$ bucket $\div$ 5 classrooms $= \frac{4}{6} \times \frac{1}{5} = \frac{4}{30} = \frac{2}{15}$ of a bucket per classroom.
Incorrect Answers:
 A. The answer was not simplified.
 C. Division was changed to multiplication, but the reciprocal of 5 ($\frac{1}{5}$) was not used.
 D. Both $\frac{4}{6}$ and 5 were replaced with their reciprocals.

71. Correct Answer: D
The chef used $\frac{1}{3}$ of the flour to make one pizza. *Of* means multiply: $\frac{1}{3} \times 4 = \frac{1}{3} \times \frac{4}{1} = \frac{4}{3} = 1\frac{1}{3}$ bags.
Incorrect Answers:
 A. The wrong operation (division) was used. ($4 \div \frac{1}{3}$)
 B. The answer was not simplified.
 C. An error occurred when simplifying the answer ($\frac{4}{3}$).

72. Correct Answer: B
Multiply the number of laps Julia swam by $\frac{5}{8}$ to find how many laps Nick swam: $5 \times \frac{5}{8} = \frac{5}{1} \times \frac{5}{8} = \frac{25}{8} = 3\frac{1}{8}$.
Incorrect Answers:
 A. The answer was not simplified.
 C. 5 was replaced with $\frac{1}{5}$ instead of with $\frac{5}{1}$.
 D. $\frac{5}{8}$ was replaced with its reciprocal ($\frac{8}{5}$) before multiplying.

Converting Measurement Units (page 78)

73. Correct Answer: B
2,000 lb. = 1 T., so 8,000 lb. $\div$ 2,000 lb. per T. = 4 T.
Incorrect Answers:
 A. Kilogram is a metric measurement and does not convert equally into customary units.
 C. 32,000 oz. = 1 T., but 8,000 lb. = 4 T.
 D. 8 T. was calculated by dividing 8,000 lb. by 1,000 lb. per T., but a ton is 2,000 lb.

74. Correct Answer: C
3 ft. = 1 yd., so 141 ft. $\div$ 3 ft. per yd. = 47 yd.
Incorrect Answers:
 A. 423 yd. was calculated by multiplying 141 ft. $\times$ 3 ft. instead of dividing 141 ft. by 3 ft.
 B. *Cm* is the wrong label.
 D. 846 in. was calculated by multiplying 6 in. per ft. $\times$ 141 ft. instead of 12 in. per ft.

75. Correct Answer: A
1 m = 100 cm, so 100 cm per m $\times$ 24 m = 2,400 cm
Incorrect Answers:
 B. 240 cm was calculated by multiplying 24 m $\times$ 10 cm per m, instead of 100 cm per m.
 C. 24,000 cm was calculated by multiplying 24 m $\times$ 1,000 cm per m, instead of 100 cm per m.
 D. 1,200 cm was calculated by multiplying 24 m $\times$ 50 cm per m, instead of 100 cm per m.

Explanations for Test C Answers *(cont.)*

76. Correct Answer: D
1 L = 1,000 mL, so 6 L × 1,000 mL per L = 6,000 mL.
Incorrect Answers:
  A. 3,000 mL was calculated by multiplying 6 L × 500 mL per L, instead of 1,000 mL per L.
  B. 600 mL was calculated by multiplying 6 L × 100 mL per L, instead of 1,000 mL per L.
  C. 12,000 mL was calculated by multiplying 6 L × 2,000 mL per L, instead of 1,000 mL per L.

Ordered Pairs *(page 79)*

77. Correct Answer: B
The circle is located at (2,7).
Incorrect Answers:
  A. The diamond is located at (0,1).
  C. The triangle is located at (9,3).
  D. The star is located at (7,2).

78. Correct Answer: C
The triangle is located at (9,3).
Incorrect Answers:
  A. The star is located at (7,2).
  B. The square is located at (6,6).
  D. The diamond is located at (0,1).

79. Correct Answer: D
Point *C* is located at (7,1).
Incorrect Answers:
  A. Point *E* is located at (1,4).
  B. Point *D* is located at (3,6).
  C. Point *B* is located at (8,4).

80. Correct Answer: B
Point *E* is located at (1,4).
Incorrect Answers:
  A. Point *A* is located at (4,1).
  C. Point *F* is located at (2,3).
  D. Point *D* is located at (3,6).

Line Plots *(page 80)*

81. Correct Answer: D
2 students wore size $10\frac{1}{2}$ (largest size) and 1 student wore $5\frac{1}{2}$ (smallest size): 2 − 1 = 1.
Incorrect Answers:
  A. 5 is the difference between the sizes ($10\frac{1}{2}$ and $5\frac{1}{2}$).
  B. 3 is the sum of students wearing the largest and smallest sizes.
  C. 2 is the number of students wearing the largest size.

82. Correct Answer: A
size $8\frac{1}{2}$ = 5 students, size 9 = 1 student, size $9\frac{1}{2}$ = 2 students, and size $10\frac{1}{2}$ = 2 students: 5 + 1 + 2 + 2 = 10 students
Incorrect Answers:
  B. 5 students includes the students that wore sizes 9, $9\frac{1}{2}$, and $10\frac{1}{2}$; it did not include size $8\frac{1}{2}$.
  C. 13 students includes the students that wore sizes $7\frac{1}{2}$; $7\frac{1}{2}$ is equal to $7\frac{1}{2}$, not greater than $7\frac{1}{2}$.
  D. 8 students is the number of students that wore shoe sizes less than $7\frac{1}{2}$, not greater than $7\frac{1}{2}$.

83. Correct Answer: B
4 students wore size $6\frac{1}{2}$.
Incorrect Answers:
  A. 5 students includes 1 student that wore size 6.
  C. 4 students wore size $6\frac{1}{2}$, not 3 students.
  D. 4 students wore size $6\frac{1}{2}$, not 6 students.

84. Correct Answer: C
$5\frac{1}{2}$ = 1 student, 6 = 1 student, $6\frac{1}{2}$ = 4 students, 7 = 2 students, $7\frac{1}{2}$ = 3 students, $8\frac{1}{2}$ = 5 students, 9 = 1 student, $9\frac{1}{2}$ = 2 students, $10\frac{1}{2}$ = 2 students: 1 + 1 + 4 + 2 + 3 + 5 + 1 + 2 + 2 = 21 students
Incorrect Answers:
  A. The number of data values was counted incorrectly.
  B. The number of data values was counted incorrectly.
  D. The number of data values was counted incorrectly.

Volume of Solid Figures *(page 81)*

85. Correct Answer: D
5 rows × 3 cubes in each row = 15 cubic units
Incorrect Answers:
  A. *Units* is the wrong label.
  B. 18 cubic units was calculated by counting the visible faces on the top and front of the object.
  C. 23 cubic units was calculated by counting all the visible faces on the object.

86. Correct Answer: B
7 cubes in each layer × 8 layers = 56 cubic units
Incorrect Answers:
  A. The wrong operation (addition) was used.
  C. 48 cubic units would be 8 layers with 6 cubes in each layer.
  D. 71 cubic units was calculated by counting all the visible faces of the object.

87. Correct Answer: A
bottom layer = 5 cubes, middle layer = 3 cubes, and top layer = 2 cubes: 5 + 3 + 2 = 10 cubic units
Incorrect Answers:
  B. 18 cubic units was calculated by counting all the visible faces.
  C. 7 cubic units was calculated by adding the bottom layer (5) and the top layer (2); it does not include the middle layer (3).
  D. 8 cubic units was calculated by adding the bottom layer (5) and the middle layer (3); it does not include the top layer (2).

88. Correct Answer: C
14 cubes in each layer × 3 layers = 42 cubic units
Incorrect Answers:
  A. 28 cubic units would be 2 layers with 14 cubes in each layer instead of 3 layers.
  B. The wrong operation (addition) was used.
  D. *Units* is the wrong label.

Volume of Rectangular Prisms *(page 82)*

89. Correct Answer: B
$V = l × w × h$: 9 ft. × 6 ft. × 2 ft. = 108 ft.^{3}
Incorrect Answers:
  A. 17 ft.^{3} was calculated by adding $l + w + h$ instead of multiplying.
  C. 54 ft.^{3} was calculated by multiplying $l × w$; h was not included.
  D. 18 ft.^{3} was calculated by multiplying $l × h$; w was not included.

Explanations for Test C Answers *(cont.)*

90. Correct Answer: B

$V = l \times w \times h$

Volume of Rectangular Prism 1 = 11 m × 7 m × 3 m = 231 m³
Volume of Rectangular Prism 2 = 5 m × 2 m × 4 m = 40 m³
Total Volume = 231 m³ + 40 m³ = 271 m³

Incorrect Answers:

A. M² is the wrong label.

C. M is the wrong label.

D. 231 m³ is the volume of rectangular prism 1; it does not include the entire figure.

91. Correct Answer: D

$V = l \times w \times h$

Volume of Rectangular Prism 1 = 5 cm × 5 cm × 2 cm = 50 cm³
Volume of Rectangular Prism 2 = 6 cm × 6 cm × 10 cm = 360 cm³
50 cm³ + 360 cm³ = 410 cm³

Incorrect Answers:

A. 360 cm³ is the volume of rectangular prism 2; it does not include the entire figure.

B. 34 cm³ was calculated by adding all the numbers together instead of multiplying to find the volume of each rectangular prism separately and then adding them together.

C. 310 cm³ was calculated by subtracting the volume of rectangular prism 1 from the volume of rectangular prism 2 instead of adding the volumes together.

92. Correct Answer: C

$V = l \times w \times h$

7 in. × 6 in. × 24 in. = 1,008 in.³

Incorrect Answers:

A. 144 in.³ was calculated by multiplying $w \times h$; l was not included.

B. 42 in.³ was calculated by multiplying $l \times w$; h was not included.

D. 37 in.³ was calculated by adding $l + w + h$ instead of multiplying $l \times w \times h$.

Area of Rectangles with Fractional Sides *(page 83)*

93. Correct Answer: B

$A = l \times w$. Convert the mixed numbers to improper fractions: $12\frac{1}{2} = \frac{25}{2}$ and $10\frac{4}{5} = \frac{54}{5}$. Cross cancel the numerator 25 with the denominator 5 and the numerator 54 with the denominator 2 to get $\frac{5}{1} \times \frac{27}{1} = \frac{135}{1} = 135$.

Incorrect Answers:

A. The answer was not simplified.

C. The whole numbers were multiplied, then the fractions were multiplied and simplified.

D. The answer was not simplified.

94. Correct Answer: D

$A = l \times w$. Convert the mixed numbers to improper fractions: $2\frac{1}{2} = \frac{5}{2}$ and $5\frac{1}{4} = \frac{21}{4}$: $\frac{5}{2} \times \frac{21}{4} = \frac{105}{8} = 13\frac{1}{8}$.

Incorrect Answers:

A. The whole numbers were multiplied, then the fractions were multiplied.

B. The mixed numbers were written as improper fractions, but the numerators were added together and the denominators were added together and simplified.

C. The answer was not simplified.

95. Correct Answer: C

$A = l \times w$. Convert the mixed numbers to improper fractions: $7\frac{1}{2} = \frac{15}{2}$ and $10\frac{2}{3} = \frac{32}{3}$. Cross cancel the numerator 15 with the denominator 3 and the numerator 32 with the denominator 2 to get $\frac{5}{1} \times \frac{16}{1} = \frac{80}{1} = 80$.

Incorrect Answers:

A. The whole numbers were multiplied, then the fractions were multiplied and simplified.

B. The answer was not simplified.

D. The answer was not simplified.

96. Correct Answer: A

$A = l \times w$. Convert the mixed numbers to improper fractions: $2\frac{2}{3} = \frac{8}{3}$ and $5\frac{1}{3} = \frac{16}{3}$: $\frac{8}{3} \times \frac{16}{3} = \frac{128}{9} = 14\frac{2}{9}$.

Incorrect Answers:

B. The answer was not simplified.

C. The whole numbers were multiplied, then the fractions were multiplied.

D. The mixed numbers were written as improper fractions, but the numerators were added together and the denominators were added together and simplified.

Classifying Two-dimensional Shapes *(page 84)*

97. Correct Answer: B

The rhombus and the square both have all sides with equal length.

Incorrect Answers:

A. A square has four right angles, but a rhombus does not.

C. A square is a rectangle because it has four right angles; a rhombus does not have four right angles, so it is not a rectangle.

D. The correct answer is B.

98. Correct Answer: D

The figure is a quadrilateral because it has four sides; it is a trapezoid because it is a quadrilateral with one pair of parallel sides.

Incorrect Answers:

A. A rhombus has four sides with equal length; this shape does not.

B. A rectangle has four right angles and two sets of parallel sides; this shape does not.

C. A square has four right angles and four sides with equal length; this shape does not.

99. Correct Answer: D

A trapezoid is not a parallelogram because both sets of opposite sides are not parallel, and it does not have all sides with equal length.

Incorrect Answers:

A. A rhombus is parallelogram with four sides of equal length.

B. A rectangle is a parallelogram.

C. A square is a parallelogram with four sides of equal length.

100. Correct Answer: D

This is a square because it has four sides of equal length and four right angles.

Incorrect Answers:

A. The figure is a parallelogram, but this is not the best answer because it has four right angles.

B. and C. The figure is a rectangle, but this is not the best answer because it has four sides of equal length and four right angles.

Bubble Answer Sheet   Test _____

1. Ⓐ Ⓑ Ⓒ Ⓓ	18. Ⓐ Ⓑ Ⓒ Ⓓ	35. Ⓐ Ⓑ Ⓒ Ⓓ	51. Ⓐ Ⓑ Ⓒ Ⓓ	68. Ⓐ Ⓑ Ⓒ Ⓓ	85. Ⓐ Ⓑ Ⓒ Ⓓ
2. Ⓐ Ⓑ Ⓒ Ⓓ	19. Ⓐ Ⓑ Ⓒ Ⓓ	36. Ⓐ Ⓑ Ⓒ Ⓓ	52. Ⓐ Ⓑ Ⓒ Ⓓ	69. Ⓐ Ⓑ Ⓒ Ⓓ	86. Ⓐ Ⓑ Ⓒ Ⓓ
3. Ⓐ Ⓑ Ⓒ Ⓓ	20. Ⓐ Ⓑ Ⓒ Ⓓ	37. Ⓐ Ⓑ Ⓒ Ⓓ	53. Ⓐ Ⓑ Ⓒ Ⓓ	70. Ⓐ Ⓑ Ⓒ Ⓓ	87. Ⓐ Ⓑ Ⓒ Ⓓ
4. Ⓐ Ⓑ Ⓒ Ⓓ	21. Ⓐ Ⓑ Ⓒ Ⓓ	38. Ⓐ Ⓑ Ⓒ Ⓓ	54. Ⓐ Ⓑ Ⓒ Ⓓ	71. Ⓐ Ⓑ Ⓒ Ⓓ	88. Ⓐ Ⓑ Ⓒ Ⓓ
5. Ⓐ Ⓑ Ⓒ Ⓓ	22. Ⓐ Ⓑ Ⓒ Ⓓ	39. Ⓐ Ⓑ Ⓒ Ⓓ	55. Ⓐ Ⓑ Ⓒ Ⓓ	72. Ⓐ Ⓑ Ⓒ Ⓓ	89. Ⓐ Ⓑ Ⓒ Ⓓ
6. Ⓐ Ⓑ Ⓒ Ⓓ	23. Ⓐ Ⓑ Ⓒ Ⓓ	40. Ⓐ Ⓑ Ⓒ Ⓓ	56. Ⓐ Ⓑ Ⓒ Ⓓ	73. Ⓐ Ⓑ Ⓒ Ⓓ	90. Ⓐ Ⓑ Ⓒ Ⓓ
7. Ⓐ Ⓑ Ⓒ Ⓓ	24. Ⓐ Ⓑ Ⓒ Ⓓ	41. Ⓐ Ⓑ Ⓒ Ⓓ	57. Ⓐ Ⓑ Ⓒ Ⓓ	74. Ⓐ Ⓑ Ⓒ Ⓓ	91. Ⓐ Ⓑ Ⓒ Ⓓ
8. Ⓐ Ⓑ Ⓒ Ⓓ	25. Ⓐ Ⓑ Ⓒ Ⓓ	42. Ⓐ Ⓑ Ⓒ Ⓓ	58. Ⓐ Ⓑ Ⓒ Ⓓ	75. Ⓐ Ⓑ Ⓒ Ⓓ	92. Ⓐ Ⓑ Ⓒ Ⓓ
9. Ⓐ Ⓑ Ⓒ Ⓓ	26. Ⓐ Ⓑ Ⓒ Ⓓ	43. Ⓐ Ⓑ Ⓒ Ⓓ	59. Ⓐ Ⓑ Ⓒ Ⓓ	76. Ⓐ Ⓑ Ⓒ Ⓓ	93. Ⓐ Ⓑ Ⓒ Ⓓ
10. Ⓐ Ⓑ Ⓒ Ⓓ	27. Ⓐ Ⓑ Ⓒ Ⓓ	44. Ⓐ Ⓑ Ⓒ Ⓓ	60. Ⓐ Ⓑ Ⓒ Ⓓ	77. Ⓐ Ⓑ Ⓒ Ⓓ	94. Ⓐ Ⓑ Ⓒ Ⓓ
11. Ⓐ Ⓑ Ⓒ Ⓓ	28. Ⓐ Ⓑ Ⓒ Ⓓ	45. Ⓐ Ⓑ Ⓒ Ⓓ	61. Ⓐ Ⓑ Ⓒ Ⓓ	78. Ⓐ Ⓑ Ⓒ Ⓓ	95. Ⓐ Ⓑ Ⓒ Ⓓ
12. Ⓐ Ⓑ Ⓒ Ⓓ	29. Ⓐ Ⓑ Ⓒ Ⓓ	46. Ⓐ Ⓑ Ⓒ Ⓓ	62. Ⓐ Ⓑ Ⓒ Ⓓ	79. Ⓐ Ⓑ Ⓒ Ⓓ	96. Ⓐ Ⓑ Ⓒ Ⓓ
13. Ⓐ Ⓑ Ⓒ Ⓓ	30. Ⓐ Ⓑ Ⓒ Ⓓ	47. Ⓐ Ⓑ Ⓒ Ⓓ	63. Ⓐ Ⓑ Ⓒ Ⓓ	80. Ⓐ Ⓑ Ⓒ Ⓓ	97. Ⓐ Ⓑ Ⓒ Ⓓ
14. Ⓐ Ⓑ Ⓒ Ⓓ	31. Ⓐ Ⓑ Ⓒ Ⓓ	48. Ⓐ Ⓑ Ⓒ Ⓓ	64. Ⓐ Ⓑ Ⓒ Ⓓ	81. Ⓐ Ⓑ Ⓒ Ⓓ	98. Ⓐ Ⓑ Ⓒ Ⓓ
15. Ⓐ Ⓑ Ⓒ Ⓓ	32. Ⓐ Ⓑ Ⓒ Ⓓ	49. Ⓐ Ⓑ Ⓒ Ⓓ	65. Ⓐ Ⓑ Ⓒ Ⓓ	82. Ⓐ Ⓑ Ⓒ Ⓓ	99. Ⓐ Ⓑ Ⓒ Ⓓ
16. Ⓐ Ⓑ Ⓒ Ⓓ	33. Ⓐ Ⓑ Ⓒ Ⓓ	50. Ⓐ Ⓑ Ⓒ Ⓓ	66. Ⓐ Ⓑ Ⓒ Ⓓ	83. Ⓐ Ⓑ Ⓒ Ⓓ	100. Ⓐ Ⓑ Ⓒ Ⓓ
17. Ⓐ Ⓑ Ⓒ Ⓓ	34. Ⓐ Ⓑ Ⓒ Ⓓ		67. Ⓐ Ⓑ Ⓒ Ⓓ	84. Ⓐ Ⓑ Ⓒ Ⓓ	